NEEDLEPOINT

A pole screen in the Metropolitan Museum of Art, New York. English mid-18th century

Hope Hanley

NEEDLEPOINT

CHARLES SCRIBNER'S SONS
NEW YORK

TITLE PAGE: On the title-page, a pair of hand screens, English, early 18th century.

To my husband,
who helped so much

CONTENTS

ACKNOWLEDGMENT

My appreciation goes to Betsy Forte and Nancy Mrozinski for their assorted suggestions and help, to Mr. James M. O'Neill of the District of Columbia Public Library and to Miss Doris Bowman of the Smithsonian Institution, as well as Mrs. Kevin Keegan of the Needlepoint Committee of the Washington Cathedral, and Mr. Charles Way of Woodlawn Plantation, and especially to my sagacious editor at Charles Scribner's Sons, Miss Elinor Parker.

INTRODUCTION

What is needlepoint? Needlepoint is counted embroidery stitches worked with a needle over the threads of a canvas. There are basically only two kinds of needlepoint stitches: short stitches covering one mesh or thread, and long stitches covering two or more mesh or threads. These two basic stitches can be handled in two different ways to form more variations. The long or the short stitches may either be "tied down" or cross themselves in some way. All needlepoint stitches trace their origin back to the two basic stitches or one or both of the variations.

This book is intended for the person who wants to do more than just fill in backgrounds of needlepoint canvases with the half cross stitch. It is intended for the person who wants to create something original, for the person who wants to use needlepoint as his personal art medium. In this book you will find designing techniques which apply to needlepoint. There are over fifty needlepoint stitches here for you to try. Experiment with them, combine them. Mix them as *you* please.

The beginning needlepointer will perhaps be hesitant to jump right in and start designing. An easy way to get the feel of "painting" with wool and to touch on the fringes of designing is to buy a professionally designed canvas which will come complete with the right amount of wool. There are also on the market some very attractive canvases with part of the design worked and the rest traméed as a design guide for the buyer. A canvas with the design already com-

A variety of articles worked in needlepoint: belts, coasters, a zippered pouch, a billfold, knitting and handbags, man's slippers

pleted would be the most economical procedure for the person who just wants to experiment with new background stitches. Any of the above suggestions will surely spark some designing ideas and you will have your first canvas designed (mentally, anyway) before you have completed your experimental piece.

To many needlepointers much of the material in this book will not be new, but perhaps it will serve as a reminder of stitches forgotten or techniques untried.

One of twelve matching chair seats

Some of the stitches in this book date back to the time of Mary, Queen of Scots. One or two were gleaned from stitchery books of a hundred years ago. The Metropolitan Museum in New York is the best source for seeing how the old stitches were once used. The National Cathedral (the seat of the Presiding Bishop of the Protestant Episcopal Church of the United States) in Washington, D. C. is the best place to see how needlepoint stitches and design can be used to-day. But don't stick to what others have done. *Experiment!* This book will show you the techniques and then you are on your own to create as you will.

CANVAS

TYPES OF CANVAS AND THEIR USES

Penelope   There are two basic types of needlepoint canvas, single thread and two thread or double thread. The two thread kind is probably better known than the single thread. It is called penelope canvas. In color it is usually ecru or an olive tan. Ten mesh to the inch is the most commonly used in penelope. All canvas is described or measured by the number of mesh per inch. Each intersection of threads is called a mesh.

Penelope canvas has two threads to work over each way, two warp threads woven quite close together and two woof threads woven a little further apart. Penelope is the kind of canvas used for the finished center canvases sold by needlework departments in large department stores. Perhaps the reason penelope is used for these canvases is because the half cross stitch works so well on it. The half cross stitch will not work at all well on the other type of canvas. Half cross stitch and the new quick point stitch are all that some people think there is to needlepoint (see p. 60). Rug canvas is generally two thread but the two threads are evenly spaced apart. If you order penelope by mail specify that you want penelope for needlepoint as there is also a penelope used for cross stitch embroidery.

Mono-canvas   Single thread canvas has many names. It is known as mono-canvas, French mono-canvas (whether it was made in France or not), uni-mesh, uni-canvas or "uni," and congress canvas. Mono-canvas is used for gros point as well as petit point. The warp thread is placed an even distance away from the woof thread. It looks like bandage gauze for a giant. Mono-canvas is usually white, though as it becomes finer in mesh it may be yellow or ecru.

All canvas is now made of cotton or Egyptian cotton. When buying canvas keep in mind the scale of your design and that the size of the mesh will affect the size of your finished piece. Reject any piece of canvas that has flaws in it such as tied threads or weak and thin-looking threads in the body of the canvas. You will be exerting quite a bit of weight on the canvas when you stretch it at completion and the weak threads might pop at that time. The more highly polished threads will take harder wear so look for a glossy finish to the canvas. It should not look floury. Most canvas has some starch in it, which makes it easier to keep the threads in place and separated while it is being worked. Rug canvas is so stiff and starchy that it almost hurts the hands to hold on to it. If the design is worth doing at all, do it well, buy the best materials you can. You don't want the museums of a hundred years from now to be full of flimsy exhibitions of needle-point, do you?

Canvas widths range from 24 inches wide to 36 inches and in some cases wider. Rug canvas is usually 36 to 40 inches wide. It comes in four and five mesh to the inch and can be bought with even fewer mesh than that. Rug canvas does not look like the usual penelope in that the two threads are evenly spaced both warp and woof, whereas regular penelope has the warp threads closer together.

The finer mesh canvases are narrower in width than the others, 24 inches wide is customary. The threads are very highly polished and made of linen or, in the case of bolting cloth, of wool. Very fine petit point is done on bolting cloth and also on gauze. Gauze starts at forty mesh to the inch and goes up to twenty-two mesh to the inch. Gauze is not flimsy, but it *is* fine, almost as fine as nylon stockings! Filoselle silk looks like rope beside it.

Gauze, laid on black paper to show texture, 40 mesh to the inch

Petit point mono-canvas, 24 mesh to the inch

Mono-canvas, 14 mesh to the inch

Penelope, 10 mesh to the inch

Rug canvas, 5 mesh to the inch

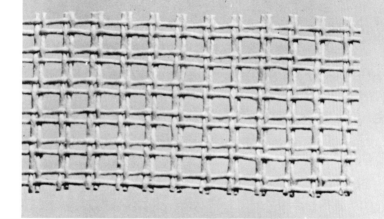

GROS POINT AND PETIT POINT

The only difference between gros point and petit point is the number of mesh per inch on the canvas on which they are done. A casual rule could be that any canvas with sixteen mesh per inch or *more* is petit point canvas, and any canvas over that up to say eight mesh per inch is gros point canvas. There is no special gros point stitch as such. The continental stitch is done on gros point canvas as well as petit point canvas and does not change its name according to the size mesh of the canvas.

Rebecca Jackson and her daughter, Susan Randolph Jackson, worked on the petit point picture together between 1820 and 1825. It was worked on fine embroidery canvas in wool. The picture is framed in applewood from a tree in the Jackson plantation.

The petit point box is called a toilet cabinet. The lid lifts up to show fitted bottles and boxes. The open door reveals several little drawers. The very fine petit point was done in silk in the second half of the seventeenth century in England.

WHAT NEEDLE FOR WHAT CANVAS?

Needles vary in size from the smallest, a size 24, to the largest, a size 15. These are the sizes commonly available today. Needlepoint needles are called tapestry needles and the best ones come from England. They come seven to a package, are large-eyed and blunt. An easy way to remember whether a needle is large or small just by the number is to keep in mind that a low number needle is used on a low number of mesh canvas, and a high number needle is used on a high number of mesh canvas. A large yarn needle is used on low mesh rug canvas.

A general guide on what needle to use with what wool and canvas would be:

Size 24 needle with 22 mesh canvas using about three strands of silk
Size 19 needle with 18 mesh canvas using crewel wool
Size 17 needle with 10 to 14 mesh canvas using Persian or tapestry wool
Size 15 needle with 8 mesh to the inch using tapestry wool or light rug wool

Since needles are so cheap one might invest in a package of 15's, 17's, 19's, and 22's or 24's, then one would be ready for any canvas. Plastic pill bottles make fine needle cases.

A kneeler of modern workmanship, in Chelsea Old Church, London; the design was adapted from Elizabethan embroideries in the Victoria and Albert Museum.

A needlepoint bag made in 1854

The other side of the bag,
showing a bargello-like pattern
worked in brick stitch

WOOL

TYPES OF WOOL REQUIRED FOR DIFFERENT CANVASES

Needlepoint wool must have long smooth fibers, therefore knitting yarns will not do because they have shorter, more wiry fibers. Most needlepoint wool sold today is moth-proofed, a real blessing. Try to stick to one brand as the weights of the wools of the same type vary; this applies to British as well as American wool. For the purposes of this book only American wools will be considered.

Crewel Wool Crewel wool is used primarily for crewel embroidery but it also makes a fine petit point wool. It is a fine springy two-ply wool. Crewel is sold in 20 to 25 yard skeins. It will work as well on ten mesh to the inch canvas (with the mesh separated to use as petit point canvas) as it will on real petit point canvas of twenty mesh to the inch.

Persian Wool Persian wool is also a two-ply wool, but it is not as springy as crewel. It is sold in three thread strands which may be worked separately or all three threads at once. Thus it is a very versatile wool in that it can be used for everything from "large" petit point to "small" rug canvas. It is convenient and economical to buy because it can be bought in small quantities, some stores even sell it by the strand! For this reason it is excellent for pictorial work, one may need only one thread of a color and it is a pity to pay the price

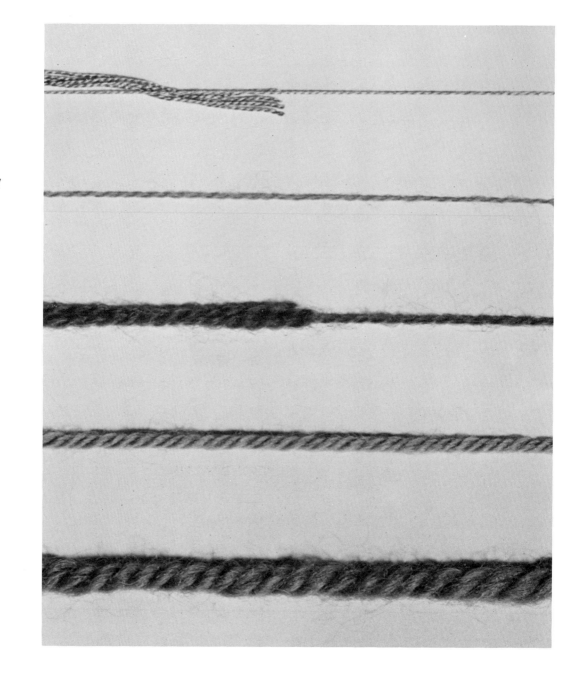

From top to bottom:
Silk, six thread strand clipped to show one thread
Crewel wool
Persian wool, three thread strand clipped to show one thread
Tapestry wool
Rug wool

of a whole 20 yard skein just for that one thread. Most professional designers sell this wool to go with their designs and include just the right amount you need to complete the design.

On very coarse canvas such as eight mesh mono-canvas, Persian can be used all three threads at once. On twelve to fourteen mesh mono-canvas one thread doubled over in the needle is used. For petit point canvas eighteen mesh, just one thread of the three thread strand is used, not doubled over. On penelope canvas ten mesh to the inch, all three threads of a strand looks best, and one thread of the three thread strand for petit point on the same canvas with the mesh separated.

Tapestry Wool   Tapestry wool is the kind sold by the department stores to finish the backgrounds of the canvases they sell. It is moth-proofed and comes in matched dye lots. It is four ply, and comes in 40 yard skeins. Needlework stores which carry Persian wool usually carry tapestry wool also. Tapestry wool can be used on twelve and fourteen mesh mono-canvas, and on ten mesh penelope with the canvas threads separated it can be used for petit point when split down to two of its four ply.

Rug Wool   Rug wool is three ply and more rough-textured than the smaller wools. It is sold by the pound which gives approximately 250 yards of wool. A scatter or strip rug will take a minimum of four pounds of wool. Rug wool is used on canvas eight mesh to the inch and lower.

Filoselle Silk   The silk most used for petit point is not made in America. This silk comes from France and England. It is sold in one and a half ounce skeins or in nine yard skeins. It is quite expensive. Silk is two-ply, fast to light and comes in six thread strands. One can use all six threads at once or as many as the canvas will bear. Silk is used on gauze, one or two threads at a time, depending on the mesh.

The shades in silk are really very lovely and quite varied. Silk is often used on faces in petit point and for highlighting. It is also used for outlining in backstitch between continental stitches to give emphasis to a certain part of a design.

Thrums   Thrums are mentioned often in British needlework books and though thrums are not sold in the United States a definition should be given under this heading. Thrums are ends of wool left over from carpet making in factories. The ends are sold in bales of

"Mary of Scotland Mourning over the Dying Douglas" from a painting by Landseer. It measures four feet by five and one half feet. The picture is one of the better examples of Berlin woolwork and was done sometime in the latter part of the 19th century. Paper patterns and bright wools from Berlin were much in vogue for needlework during the Victorian era, hence the name Berlin woolwork.

A tiny bunch of violets worked in silk on fine gauze.

mixed colors. A short pile needle is used on a string rug canvas. Most British writers deplore the use of thrums for good needlework.

HOW TO FIGURE WOOL REQUIREMENTS

First you must measure the length and width of the area of canvas you wish to cover. If you are figuring background wool, measure the subject's length and width so that you can subtract an approximate amount from the total. Multiply the length by the width in *inches*. Then multiply this total by the number of inches of wool it takes to

above and opposite: Two chair seats worked by H. M. Queen Mary, now in the Metropolitan Museum.

Note the signature and dates in the lower right-hand corners, which add historical interest.

cover one square inch of canvas. (The yardage for each stitch is given in the section devoted to the fancy stitches. If your wool and canvas are different from those used in the stitch section you will have to do a one inch square test patch for your specific requirements.) Then divide your total by 36 to convert back to yards.

As aforementioned, some wool is sold by strands, such as Persian wool. These strands are approximately 1¾ yards long. They contain three threads. If you are using just a single thread in the needle you will average about 5 yards of wool for each full strand. If you are using all three threads in the needle at once, you will get just 1¾ yards per strand. When buying wool by the pound you must know just how many yards there are per pound.

Here is an example of how the wool requirement for a rug 36 by 36 inches would be calculated. It takes 15 inches of rug wool to cover one square inch of five mesh to the inch rug canvas in the half cross stitch. First multiply the length by the width: $36 \times 36 = 1296$. Then multiply this figure by the number of inches of wool it takes to cover one square inch of canvas, $15 \times 1296 = 19,440$. To reconvert this to yards divide this total by 36. $36 \div 19440 = 540$ yards, the answer. Now in Paternayan's rug yarn there are about 270 yards per pound. As 270 and 270 equal 540, you would need exactly two pounds of rug wool.

To give a general idea of how much wool is needed for various mesh canvases here are some random requirements:

To cover one square inch of eighteen mesh mono-canvas, it takes 2 yards and 4 inches of Persian wool used single thread doing the continental stitch. The requirement would be the same if crewel wool were substituted.

To cover one square inch of ten mesh penelope canvas, it takes 30 inches of tapestry wool doing the half cross stitch.

To cover one square inch of twenty-four mesh uni-canvas it takes 3⅔ yards of Filoselle silk, using only three threads of the six thread strand in continental stitch.

FRAMES

Many experienced needlepointers prefer to hold their work in a frame. Some of the fancy stitches go much faster in a frame simply because you don't have to support the canvas yourself, thus freeing both hands to do the stitch, one from the top of the canvas, and one underneath. Frames are a must for rug-making, you just can't hold all that weight comfortably in one hand.

Floor frames and some hand frames work on the scroll principle,

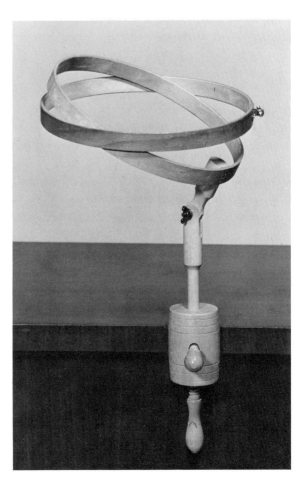

An embroidery hoop attached to a sewing bird which clamps to the table.

A rotating frame. Note the webbing attached to the long bars.

the scroll rods being held in place and taut by screw rods. Sometimes the scroll rods are held in place by clamps on the side rods. The simplest frames use pegs to hold the rods in place. The canvas is attached to the frame by webbing or direct tacking to the scroll rod, and as it is finished the completed part is rolled on to the bottom scroll rod exposing more unworked canvas coming from the top scroll rod. One can lace the sides of the canvas to the vertical rods with cord or with lacing kits which can be purchased. This will make the whole canvas more taut and rigid. When completely mounted and laced the frame and canvas will look like a little trampolin.

The floor frames come from England in 24 and 36 inch sizes. That means that they will accommodate canvas 24 and 36 inches wide. The frames come nicely finished and stained, suitable for setting up in your living room. For half the price of one of the English frames one can buy a less finished piece of furniture but just as adequate a frame. This would be a rug-hooking frame which can be purchased in any store that carries rug-hooking supplies. They are, of course, rather large, 36 to 40 inches wide. They work on the same principle as the imports, the only difference being that the wood is unfinished. They do not have a webbing attached. If you would rather not tack the canvas right to the horizontal scroll rods, just buy half a yard of heavy muslin or a similar material, cut it in half and tack a strip to both the bottom and top horizontal rods, from the very edge to the very edge. With heavy duty thread turn down a one inch hem on your needlepoint canvas at each end. Sew the hemmed part by hand to the webbing, top and bottom.

A standing embroidery frame which belonged to Nelly Custis Lewis. Note the baskets for wool on the main posts. Mrs. Lewis was working on the piece of work in the frame at the time of her death. The frame stands in the upstairs sitting room of her former home, Woodlawn Plantation, Mount Vernon, Virginia.

Another type of frame is the rotating frame. It is just like the standing variety except that it is smaller and has no stand. To use the rotating frame you brace it against a chair or table with your body, you then have both hands free to work. The canvas is mounted on the frame the same way. The advantage of the rotating frame is that it can be turned around as it is worked. It is used on smaller canvases. Another type of frame is the embroidery hoop fitted up with a sewing bird. A sewing bird is a vise-like holder which clamps to the table. One could put quite small canvases in a hoop. The embroidery hoop is the least desirable of the frames, it stretches the canvas out of shape where it is being held and any piece that will fit in an embroidery hoop is small enough to be held in the hand. The main reasons for using a frame are because the canvas is too bulky to be held by hand, and because frames do keep the canvas from stretching sideways out of shape as you work.

If you are doing straight needlepoint, and no fancy stitches, a frame will just make your work go slower. The straight needlepoint stitches take just one thrust to go in and out of the canvas. On a frame the canvas would be too taut to receive the needle this way and you would have to put your hand underneath to receive it and to thrust it back up. However, on many of the fancy stitches one has to move the hand over and under the canvas whether you are using a frame or not, so that the frame would make it easier because one hand could stay on top and the other underneath sending the needle back and forth.

A winged chair in lozenge design in the Governor's Palace, Williamsburg, Virginia. English c.1720

DESIGN

SOURCES OF DESIGN

Your home is a wonderful source of design ideas. A design from the upholstery of one piece of furniture can be selected and used elsewhere on a cushion or a seatcover. Perhaps there is a repeat design in your drapery material that could be used as a single motif on a foot stool. Part of the pattern of the rug could be copied or even the trim on the fireplace. One small part of a large design could be framed in squares in a checkered design or as a repeat design all by itself. Wall paper designs make fine repeat motifs. Stripes and plaids can be created from the colors used in a room and different fancy stitches can be used to define them. Damask table linen is a good source for dining room chair designs. Pick just one flower design from the dining room rug and repeat it for the chair seats.

Textiles in museums can suggest repeat patterns too. Jacquard designs in particular adapt well to needlepoint because the patterns for Jacquard are designed to be executed stitch by stitch. For designs to be used on cushions, book covers, vests or just as pictures one can use one's hobbies and interests laid out on a plain background. Book illustrations or religious symbols supply design ideas. Doing the family coat of arms is a good idea except that once the relatives see it they will want one. Club emblems and school crests are ideas too. Cross-stitch embroidery books have quite a few adaptable ideas in them. Representations of your home, your pets, favorite flowers and fruits, sports and clubs could be combined or used separately.

A side chair with the small fruits worked in petit point.

A Chippendale child's chair, only 10 inches across the back and 11 inches on the other sides; the heads of some of the animals are in petit point.

38

Design

A chair in the Governor's Palace, Williamsburg, upholstered in petit point in a lightly colored floral design.

A chair seat made by Sarah
Tyler in Boston, 1740.

A view of the Crystal Palace,
London, site of The Great
Exhibition of 1851, worked in
silk and wool.

Another source of ideas is period furniture, a history of which will not appear here. Period furniture is best seen, not read about, and for design purposes should really not be followed too slavishly. After all, you can buy period canvases already designed, why design what you can buy? Needlepoint went from Cluny-type design (flowers, plants and animals scattered at random on a dark background) to pictorials set in strapping or cartouche, then back to an over-all pattern and finally to large florals. Dark backgrounds predominated in the 16th and 17th century but with the advent of the famous furniture designers of the Georgian period backgrounds became lighter and lighter. The French always seemed to prefer lighter or brighter backgrounds. Bargello was used throughout all of the periods, the original idea coming from the Orient.

The author's first attempt at designing needlepoint: her children and her pets.

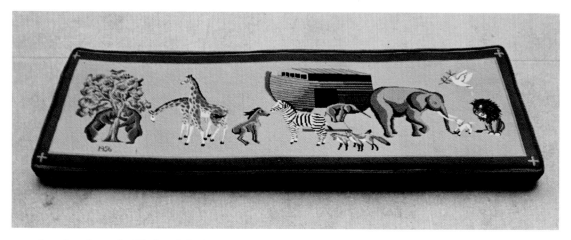

Two kneelers from the National Cathedral, Washington, D. C.

ABOVE: from the Children's Chapel

BELOW: from the Bethlehem Chapel

The point of embroidery is to represent objects in stylized form. One should not be photographically realistic in designing needlepoint. On your first designing attempts, keep it simple, fancy effects and detail will come later. Don't try to put in every shadow and every nuance of color. You don't have to stick to conventional designs in needlepoint, it lends itself very well to today's modern design. Non-realistic nature forms with bold mass color effects are very handsome done in needlepoint. Just blocks of color or great poppy-like flowers on a solid background can be very effective for pillows or rugs.

Bold design is just right for the use of the fancy stitches, but if the important thing in a design is detail, don't use fancy stitches! Detail in design demands the use of the half cross stitch. Fancy stitches can create special effects in the body or subject of your design. Used in the right proportion to the main design fancy stitches make a fine backgrounding. The kneelers at the Washington Cathedral are a good example of the use of fancy stitches as a backgrounding. The main motif in each one is bold and simple with the upright Gobelin stitch, the slanting Gobelin stitch, the Scotch stitch, and an enlarged Hungarian embroidery stitch used as the backgrounding.

Have some idea of the general outline of your finished product before you begin designing so that everything will fit into the space allowed and there will not be too much space left on the top or bottom. You don't want it to look as if the design had shrunk after it was finished.

Don't be afraid of color. Use as bright colors as you wish, they will look darker worked up on the canvas. The colors which look bright, even gaudy on the counter, will team up quite tamely on the canvas. If you want a contrast using two shades of the same color, really contrast them. If the contrast is too subtle the colors will look almost the same shade on the canvas.

Keep in mind while laying out your colors what your background color is going to be, this applies to pictorial canvases as well as abstract. You may need a black outline on a figure if there will not be enough contrast with the immediate background color. Sometimes a much lighter shade of the same color as the subject will work, for instance, a light grey outline on a dark grey hippopotamus who is standing on a dark green field. A black outline would be lost in a situation such as this. Some needlepointers prefer to outline with black Filoselle silk when the canvas is finished, making a little back stitch between the other stitches, but this method is apt to look like an afterthought if not carefully handled. When doing landscapes remember that the darker colors are used in the foreground and the lighter shades beyond for distance.

When it comes to framing needlepoint pictures one rarely uses a mat, especially a paper one, so to make a picture canvas look more "finished" one can make a border of fancy stitches around the edge or a border of half cross stitch in another color. The wood frame will go around this. When doing a needlepoint coat of arms border it or ask your framer to put a gold liner on the inside edge of the frame. A gold border painted on the glass is very elegant but it is also very expensive.

Unless you are designing something that is absolutely flat modern or primitive you will want to have a little depth in your figures. Use three shades of the same color wool to achieve depth in clothing on human figures, the outside edge of the clothing should be darker shades of the rest of the garment. For skin and hair the darker shade would again go on the outside edge, two shades will suffice. Even if you only outline the faces in a darker shade of pink, it will add definition. Animals require only two shades.

For trees you will need three shades of green, the lightest will go on the top of the tree where the sun strikes first, then darker, with the darkest on the bottom where the leaves are presumably in shadow. The first two greens can be used this way on individual branches, with the middle green being used more and more as you come closer to

Two kneelers from the Bethlehem Chapel of the National Cathedral, Washington, D. C. The background color of all the kneelers in the chapel is dark red.

Miss Kathy Price of Kensington, Maryland, drew some animals when she was nine years old. Her father, Douglas Price, M.D., transferred the pictures to canvas.

Kathy stitched the animals, her father filled in the background with the Parisian embroidery stitch. The background and frame are both grey, very effective with the dark border. The piece is entitled "Number 7."

A winged chair in the Governor's Palace, Williamsburg, Virginia. English c.1715

the bottom branches and finally the dark green taking over completely. Three shades of grey or brown are used for the tree trunks, the lightest towards the sun, the darkest towards the shadow. To make a gradual transition of color on the tree trunk, you might try splitting the ply of the two colors you want to combine. Use half a piece of each together as one complete thread.

For great detail one can use petit point on the same canvas as gros point but only on penelope canvas (as opposed to one thread or mono-canvas). To do petit point on penelope canvas just separate the two warp threads and the two woof threads and use it as one would mono-canvas. The petit point will thus be one quarter the size of the gros point stitches. You will see this done on antique needle-point in museums, especially for faces in pictorial canvases. One can add petit point to mono-canvas by insetting or appliquéing a piece of petit point canvas or gauze.

There are two methods of appliquéing, first the obvious one of sewing in the appliqué, and the other of tying it in. The sewing method is recommended for the finer meshes and for pieces of canvas which are of a widely different size mesh. Tying in is very hard on the eyes and should not be attempted for anything under fourteen mesh to the inch. Designing for appliqué is quite difficult. Keep detail on the outside outline of the appliqué to an absolute minimum, make curves gradual. Corners are not to be feared as they can be mitred. The instructions for appliquéing are to be found in a later chapter.

METHODS OF TRANSFERRING THE DESIGN TO CANVAS

There are two schools of thought on the best way to transfer design to canvas: graph paper charts versus painting on canvas. For the novice designer the graph paper method of laying out a design is the most foolproof way as well as the most educational way. You can see just what the design will look like blocked out stitch by stitch. Curves are easier to handle and errors easier to correct. You are less apt to go in for hair by hair realism on graph paper because it does have to be blocked out stitch by stitch.

Needlepoint looks best when used for mass rather than detail. As you grow more proficient at designing you will add more detail, particularly if you try your hand at a petit point piece where there is more room for detail. Some people find it is easier on their eyes to look at the graph paper design rather than two shades of the same color, that is, the painted canvas with the same shade wool on top.

On the other hand, a canvas with the design painted on it is much more portable for working on wherever you like. The graph paper method needs to be done at home where you can concentrate on counting off your design. Perhaps it boils down to whether you want to think about the needlepoint as you do it or not. If you have had some experience with painting by all means use the painted canvas method; otherwise, try the graph paper way first.

Graph Paper   The school variety of graph paper is the simplest to use because it has the squares already counted off into fives or tens. Each square counts as one stitch. If the size of your finished product

On the left, a simple sketch; on the right,

the result squared out on graph paper

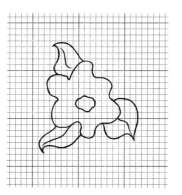 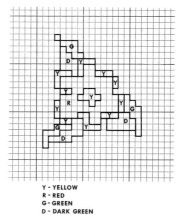

Y - YELLOW
R - RED
G - GREEN
D - DARK GREEN

is limited draw its outline in pencil on the canvas. Count the number of meshes from right to left inside the outline, and the number from top to bottom. Count off the same number of squares, right to left, top to bottom, on the graph paper and draw your outline on it. It does not matter if the scale is different, it's the mesh number that counts.

Sketch your design right on the graph paper as though it had no cross hatching on it. Then, following the lines of your sketch, block in the stitches, by the square, keeping as close to the sketch line as possible. Color the pattern with colored pencils or colored inks. To start work on the canvas you must count off the mesh to find the exact center and mark it with lead pencil (ink might run into a light wool when the canvas is wet for stretching). Find the exact center on your graph design. Start work right in the center of the canvas, working out to the edges.

A graph paper design using five colors

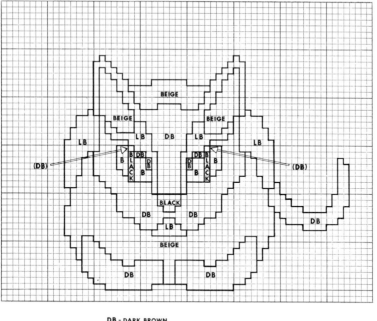

DB - DARK BROWN
LB - LIGHT BROWN
B - BLUE

Painting on the Canvas   Before you can lay brush or pencil to canvas you must do one or two things to prepare it. Assuming that you have a definite size in mind for the finished product, it helps immeasurably to mark out the outline in pencil before you start painting. Be sure you leave a margin of one and a half to two inches around the edge of the canvas, you will need it later in the finishing process. Incidentally, if you are making a chair seat, measure how high the padding rises from the frame and add that much to all the sides of your canvas. You want the finished product to fit.

Having cleared up those details, we can consider the various ways of transferring the design to the canvas before we can even start to paint. Professional designers draw the outline of their design on tracing paper or lay-out paper in india ink. Then they lay the canvas over the outline which shows up through the mesh. They are in effect tracing the design in their oil paints. This is probably the easiest looking method and the one that takes the most skill. If you have painted before perhaps this is the method to use, but you were warned, it takes considerable artistic skill.

A very primitive way of transferring the design to the canvas is to lay the design over the canvas and then prick through the paper with a lead pencil, thereby marking the canvas with little lead dots. Follow the dot to dot pattern with a heavier lead line or with oil paint. This method is unsatisfactory if your design is at all intricate.

If you are doing an abstract modern design or a still life arrangement the paper template method works very well. Make a paper cutout of each object or shape that will go into the design. Use colored construction paper, if possible, to get some idea of how the colors will show up on your finished canvas. Move the cutouts around until the design pleases you. Outline the designs right on the canvas after pinning the papers into place so that they won't slip while you are tracing around their edges.

Making a carbon paper sandwich is another method. First lay out the canvas on a firm surface, then put the carbon paper on

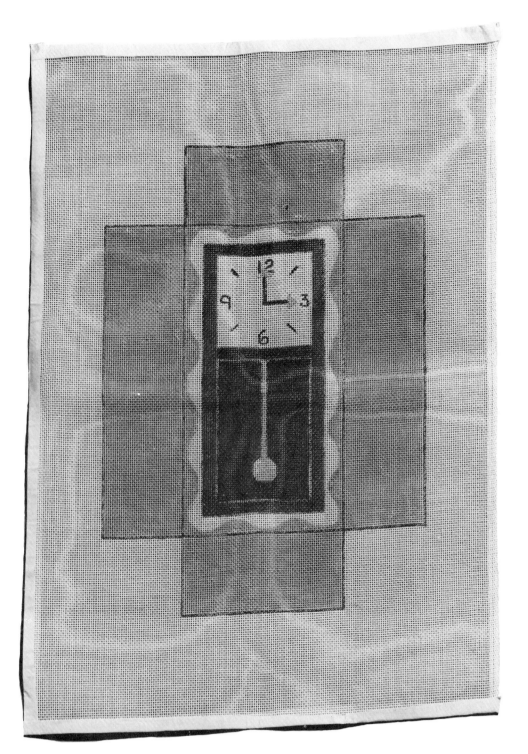

A painted canvas. The sides of this doorstop design would be sewn on completion, and felt would be rabbit-skinned to the bottom.

it, carbon side down, and lay your design on top. Tack the whole sandwich down to prevent slipping. Trace over your design with a sharpish pencil bearing down fairly heavily. Remove the design and carbon paper and slip a piece of white paper under the canvas. The white paper will help you to see the carbon outline on the canvas while you pencil or paint it in.

For very bold designs one can use wax crayons directly on the canvas. To set the colors iron lightly. The pink transfer pencil used so much in crewel work designing does not work for needlepoint. The canvas is just too coarse, even petit point weight won't "take" it.

If one wanted to take a design directly from a book or something else that one would not want to destroy during the designing process, a plastic overlay is the answer. A plastic overlay or drafting film looks like a piece of transparent graph paper. It can be obtained at a draftsmen's supply store. The plastic is ruled off into one inch squares over the smaller cross-hatching. Lay it over the design. Your design will then be divided into one inch squares by the grid. On your piece of canvas draw in pencil the same size squares. Then square by square draw the contents of each design square into the corresponding canvas square. If you want to make a few little changes in the design, transfer the design to paper first and then use one of the above methods to transfer from paper to canvas. The plastic overlay is used to enlarge or reduce a design by simply drawing the canvas squares larger or smaller as you wish. Of course, you can have the job of reducing or enlarging a design done by photostat processing.

If you plan to take your design from a rug or something so large that the plastic overlay would not work, and wish to reduce the size of the design anyway, you can still use the overlay idea in principle. Stake the area out with pins and then wrap thread from pin to pin to make a cross hatching or grid. From there you would draw square by square onto your canvas as you did before. Spaghetti (uncooked, of course) scotch-taped down over the design will form the desired grid too. The plastic overlay has still another use. It can be used just like a piece of real graph paper. Lay the plastic over the design, trace it, color it with colored pencils and go to work counting off the stitches from the plastic.

All of the above methods of transferring would be followed up by painting in the colors with oil paint or as mentioned with wax crayons. The design can be more sharply defined on mono-canvas than on penelope. One can use paint on petit point canvas but it must be used thinly, otherwise it will clog the fine mesh. Oil paints are the most satisfactory to use on any canvas. India ink and egg oil emul-

A design idea taken with few changes from a greeting card. The cross stitch, leaf stitch, Byzantine stitch, and interlocking Gobelin stitch were used on the rooster.

sion tempera have the same fault in common: running when wet. When the canvas is finished, it must be wet to stretch it back into shape. This cancels the use of any medium that is not waterproof. Ink and tempera run, not just into the wool on top of it but into the adjoining stitches. Casein shares the running disadvantage to a lesser degree, but it *does* run. It also smells even when dry and thus is not very pleasant to work over.

Oil paint may be used directly from the tube, but it will take forever to dry if used that way. A few drops of Japan dryer in your paint will have the canvas dry in twenty-four hours. Japan dryer can be obtained from any art supply store. Mix in just a few drops. It will darken the color just a little. If you can wait a little longer before setting needle to canvas try turpentine as the drying agent. Use half as much turpentine as you have paint. Your mixture will be about the consistency of cream. This combination will dry in forty-eight hours.

Paint with a fine brush. Use the paint sparingly until you know how to handle it. Needlepoint canvas is no place for impasto, it will clog the mesh with paint. You should use so little paint that none will come through on the other side or at least very little. Finally, be sure the canvas is completely dry before you start to work with your needle.

THE STITCHES

All of the stitches in this book were tested on fourteen mesh to the inch mono-canvas. The reason being that the stitches, most of them anyway, seem to fit this mesh very comfortably, they are not too loose or too tight. The few that can only be done on penelope canvas were tested on ten mesh to the inch canvas for the above reason also.

In the text of each stitch will be found the wool requirement for fourteen mesh mono-canvas or ten mesh penelope, and the type of wool used (usually Persian wool). This information was included to give the reader some idea of the relative amount of wool needed for each stitch, whether a stitch is economical of wool or a "wool-eater." The measurement given will, of course, not apply to any other canvas or wool, but it will give the reader an approximate idea of wool consumption. Persian wool was used for most of the stitches because its versatile three-thread strands can be used in any stitch situation and still be a consistent measurement.

The single thread mentioned in the stitch description means that one thread of a three thread strand of Persian wool has been used in the needle, undoubled. When it says single thread doubled over it means that the single thread of a three thread strand has been used in the needle, doubled over so that the ends are even and two threads are actually covering each mesh. If the stitch description does not say which canvas to try the stitch on, it is to be assumed that mono-canvas is preferred. The stitch will probably work on penelope but not as well as on mono-canvas. If in doubt, experiment.

In the diagrams each number signifies that the needle is going into the canvas or coming out. Just put your needle in at #1 and out at #2 and so forth.

The most efficient way to learn the stitches is to do them. Then you can see just how they will look for your design purposes. Seeing a picture or diagram in a book just does not tell the relative size to other stitches or the contrasting texture. Making a sampler is really an excellent way to make these discoveries. It is also a permanent record of the stitches which you are not apt to give away as you will give away other finished items. All you need to make a sampler is half a yard or less of both kinds of canvas, a needle and about four ounces of wool.

An 18 or 19 needle will work very well if you use fourteen mesh mono-canvas or ten mesh penelope. After cutting the canvas to size, bind the edges with masking tape so that no unravelling will occur, or turn back a little hem and hand stitch or machine stitch it down. Some people prefer to sew very wide binding tape on the cut edges. The canvas selvages are always on the sides of your work. Mark off in pencil little one-inch squares all in a row or at random. It is a good idea to leave some bare canvas around each sample if you intend to use it for future reference, and you will want to mark in ink a code or number to each stitch to identify it. You will find as you work along that design ideas will suggest themselves to you, so write them down, you'll surely forget them otherwise.

Wool wears out from being pulled through the canvas too many times. The result of this is uneven looking work. At the beginning of the thread the stitches are fat and springy, at the end of a worn-out thread the stitches are thin and flat. Use a foot of wool in your needle for petit point, about eighteen inches single or double thread for the middle range of mesh, and two feet of rug wool on rug canvas.

To start any stitch you insert the needle on the right side about an inch from the place where you really mean to start but in the path

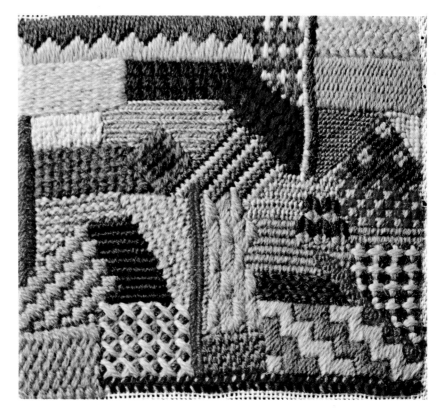

A tiny sampler incorporating 30 different stitches

A pillow with the background
worked in the knotted stitch

From the number of initials on the motif sampler it would appear that a group of friends all took part in making it. Many colors were used in the figures, the background is black, and the stitch is the half cross.

of your intended stitches. Then bring the needle up at the real starting point. Pull the wool almost through the canvas, leaving just a little tag sticking up on the front of the canvas. As you stitch, make an effort to work over that piece of wool on the back of the canvas so that it will be firmly lashed down. Pull the little tag left in front through to the back when you feel the back piece has been secured sufficiently. Never start by knotting the wool!

If your piece of canvas is large and you find it cumbersome to hold, roll up the sides as you would a scroll. Pin the rolls near the top and bottom, being careful not to split a canvas thread with the pin. Leave three or four inches unrolled in the center where you are going to work. Unpin and reroll as you work.

Keep the tension on your wool as even as you can. Uneven tension in needlepoint shows up just as much as it does in knitting. Stitches that are too tight will allow bare canvas to show through, stitches that are consistently too tight will pull the canvas way out of shape, beyond repair by stretching. When your canvas is finished and you find an occasional loose stitch here and there, just pull on the back of the stitch with your needle to draw up the slack.

To finish off a thread, run the needle through the just completed stitches on the back of the canvas, about an inch will do. The reason for finishing off a thread on its own completed stitches is to minimize trouble if ever you should need to snip out a mistake. Cut the completed thread close to the canvas. Keep the back of your canvas as neat as possible, otherwise you will be stitching in bits of color from the back to the front from nearby tag ends. The thread you are working with is apt to get snarled with tag ends from the back if they are not clipped close.

Two of the following stitches have tramé as a base. It might be well to explain now just what it is. Some canvases are sold with the background and possibly the subject done in a long horizontal basting-like stitch. This is tramé. It is used on these canvases to show what colors to use and to indicate the design. The right amount of wool and the right colors of wool are included with this type of canvas as

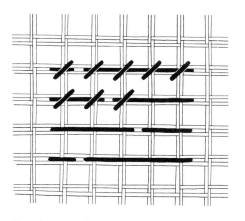

Tramé on penelope canvas

a sort of kit. One stitches right over the tramé as though it were not even there. It is an understitching. It must be laid on in irregular series, as it will form ridges if done in regular rows. Tramé may also be used to add body to a stitch, to beef it up, and this is its purpose with the stitches included here. To figure the extra wool needed to tramé, just halve the number of mesh per inch of the canvas you are using and add two inches to the figure for each square inch. Thus if you are using fourteen mesh canvas, half of fourteen is seven plus the two added inches equals nine extra inches of wool for each square inch of tramé.

The following table lists suggested uses for the stitches. It is just a guide line for you to follow until you are familiar enough with the stitches to make your own judgments on them. The word filling means a stitch to be used in an enclosed area, not the background.

In all the following stitch diagrams *odd* numbers indicate that the needle comes *up* through the canvas, *even* numbers indicate that the needle goes *down*.

APPROPRIATE USES FOR STITCHES

	filling	back-ground	striking pattern by itself	detail	slow to work up	quick to work up
Rep stitch	×	·	·	×	×	·
Cross stitch	×	·	·	×	×	·
Cross stitch tramé	×	·	×	·	×	·
Oblong cross stitch	×	×	·	·	·	×
Oblong cross stitch with back stitch	·	×	·	·	×	·
Upright cross stitch	×	×	·	×	·	×
Smyrna cross stitch	·	·	×	·	×	·
Double cross stitch	×	·	×	·	·	×
Double stitch	·	×	×	·	·	×
Rice stitch	·	·	×	·	×	·
Double straight cross stitch	·	·	×	·	·	×
Double leviathan stitch	·	·	×	·	·	×
Triple leviathan stitch	·	·	×	·	·	×
Star stitch	·	·	×	·	×	·
Diamond eyelet stitch	·	·	×	·	×	·
Straight Gobelin stitch	×	×	·	·	·	×
Renaissance stitch	×	×	·	·	·	×
Slanting Gobelin stitch	×	×	·	·	·	×
Interlocking Gobelin stitch	×	×	·	×	·	×
Encroaching oblique stitch	×	×	·	·	·	×
Plaited Gobelin stitch	×	×	×	·	·	×
Brick stitch	×	×	×	·	·	×
Parisian embroidery stitch	·	×	×	·	·	×
Hungarian embroidery stitch	·	×	×	·	·	×
Bargello stitch	×	×	×	·	·	×
Old Florentine stitch	·	·	×	·	·	×
Mosaic stitch	×	×	×	×	·	×
Scotch stitch	×	×	×	·	·	×
Cashmere stitch	×	×	×	·	·	×

	filling	background	striking pattern by itself	detail	slow to work up	quick to work up
Triangle stitch	·	·	×	·	·	×
Mosaic stitch done diagonally	×	×	×	×	·	×
Cashmere stitch done diagonally	×	×	×	·	·	×
Milanese stitch	·	×	×	·	·	×
Byzantine stitch	·	×	×	·	·	×
Scotch stitch done diagonally	×	×	×	·	·	×
Knotted stitch	×	×	·	·	·	×
French stitch	·	×	×	·	×	·
Rococo stitch	·	·	×	·	×	·
Web stitch	×	·	·	×	×	·
Chain stitch	×	·	·	×	×	·
Knitting stitch	×	×	·	×	×	·
Kalem stitch	×	×	·	×	×	·
Herringbone stitch (both)	×	×	×	·	on fine mesh	×
Two-color herringbone stitch	·	×	×	·	×	·
Oblique Slav stitch	·	×	·	·	·	×
Fern stitch	×	×	·	×	·	×
Long and short oblique stitch	·	×	×	·	·	×
Stem stitch	×	·	×	·	·	×
Perspective stitch	·	×	×	·	·	×
Greek stitch	·	×	·	×	·	×
Railway stitch	·	×	·	×	×	·
Leaf stitch	·	×	×	·	·	×
Darning stitch	·	·	×	·	×	·
Surrey stitch	×	×	·	×	·	×

I *THE HALF CROSS STITCH*

The half cross stitch takes approximately 1½ yards of Persian wool, single thread doubled over in the needle, to cover 1 square inch of penelope canvas.

There are several different ways of producing the basic short needle-point stitch. The most commonly known is the half cross stitch. It can be done only on penelope canvas because it will slide unless it has the double threads of penelope to hold it in place. Try the stitch on a piece of mono-canvas and you will understand. The half cross stitch does not provide much of a backing on the reverse side of the canvas. It also will pull the canvas out of shape somewhat. This will mean more pulling and tugging when it comes to stretching it at completion.

The half cross stitch is always done from left to right; when one row is done, turn the canvas around and work back on the next row of mesh from left to right. Your needle will be going under the woof threads of the canvas. To do the simplified half cross stitch or "quick point," you do the same thing with the needle, only it will be going under the warp threads. It is really the same stitch as the half cross except that it is worked up and down the canvas instead of from left to right.

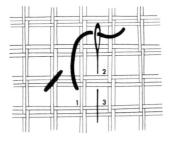

THE HALF CROSS STITCH

The continental stitch takes 3¾ yards of Persian wool, single thread doubled over, to cover 1 square inch of fourteen mesh mono-canvas.

The continental stitch is preferred by most needlepointers for filling out designs. The continental stitch works equally well on both canvases. It is the stitch used for petit point. It provides a good backing on the reverse side of the canvas which means that it will take heavier wear. The continental stitch is worked from right to left, as with the half cross stitch you must keep turning the canvas around as you work on it. When used over a large area it pulls the canvas out of shape quite a bit. The damage is not permanent, the piece can be stretched back into shape at completion, but a stiffener is recommended to help it stay in shape.

THE CONTINENTAL STITCH

III   *THE BASKET WEAVE STITCH or Bias Tent Stitch and THE DIAGONAL STITCH*

To cover 1 square inch of fourteen mesh mono-canvas, it takes
3⅔ yards of Persian wool, single thread doubled over.

The basket weave stitch is the background filler stitch. It has two advantages over the previous stitches; (1) it does not pull the canvas out of shape, and (2) you can work the stitch without having to turn the canvas around and around. Its only disadvantage is that it is not very

THE BASKET WEAVE STITCH, going up
the canvas or from right to left

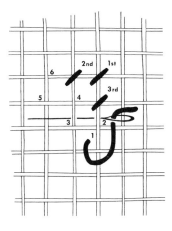

THE BASKET WEAVE STITCH, going down
the canvas or from left to right

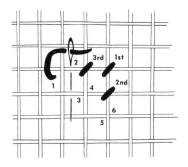

good for working out designs, it lacks maneuverability, but it does fill in large areas very efficiently and pleasantly. You must make sure that your wool is fat enough for this stitch; if it is too thin a diagonal line will show, detracting from the canvas as a whole. The basket weave stitch has a firm backing which looks as if it had been woven, hence its name. It can be worked on both canvases.

The diagonal stitch is the same thing as the basket weave stitch except that it is worked only from right to left or from top to bottom. The basket weave stitch can be worked back and forth from top to bottom and then bottom to top. The only way to tell them apart is by looking on the back of the canvas, the basket weave has that woven look and the diagonal will have diagonal ridges.

IV   *THE REP STITCH or the Aubusson Stitch*

It takes 2⅙ yards of Persian wool, single thread doubled over, to cover 1 square inch of ten mesh penelope canvas.

You might call this half a stitch. It can be done only on penelope canvas, over one of the horizontal or woof threads instead of both of them. It crosses over both of the warp or vertical threads. The result has the look of rep silk.

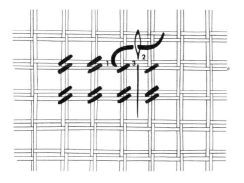

THE REP STITCH

To cover 1 square inch of fourteen mesh mono-canvas, it takes
2⅔ yards of Persian wool, single thread *not* doubled over.

The cross stitch was much used by our ancestors for their pictorial
needlepoint pictures, it was also a favorite of early English needlepointers. The cross stitch can be worked on both canvases. There is
only one thing you must be careful about and that is to make sure all
the crosses cross in the same direction, otherwise a very ragged
appearance is produced. On penelope canvas you can do the half
cross stitch from left to right and then come back on the same line
doing the half cross stitch backwards, crossing your half crosses as
you come, so to speak. On mono-canvas each stitch should be completed before going on to the next since the half cross stitch does not
make a neat looking stitch on mono-canvas. On either canvas the
amount of wool used will be the same. Don't forget to make all the
crosses cross in the same direction.

There are several variations of this stitch, but this is the one on
which they are all based.

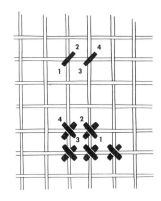

THE CROSS STITCH

The first step of the cross stitch

The second step of the cross stitch

To cover 1 square inch of fourteen mesh mono-canvas, it takes 3½ yards of Persian wool, single thread doubled over. This figure includes the tramé.

Cross stitch from a distance looks very much like plain old half cross stitch, a cross stitch tramé cannot be mistaken this way. It sits up on its understitching and the cross is quite obvious. It is appropriate to use when a fine texture is not required. When doing the tramé understitching do be sure that you are *not* doing it evenly. Make some of your long stitches over five warp threads, then over six and seven. It is important not to have a pattern of tramé stitches showing through the cross stitches. This cross stitch is the same as the one before except that it is done over two mesh each way. Don't forget to make all the crosses in the same direction.

65

Stitches

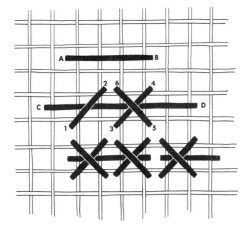

THE CROSS STITCH TRAMÉ. Letters show the tramé; numbers show the cross stitch

VII *THE OBLONG CROSS STITCH*

It takes 4⅛ yards of Persian wool, single thread doubled over,
to cover 1 square inch of fourteen mesh mono-canvas.

The oblong cross stitch is a tall cross stitch which can be done on both canvases. On mono-canvas it looks a little like rope, on penelope the crosses are more obvious. It is a hard stitch to keep uniform, the crosses tend to straggle unless the tension is even on each stitch. This stitch does not provide much of a backing. Don't forget to make all the crosses in the same direction.

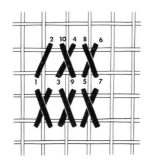

THE OBLONG CROSS STITCH

THE OBLONG CROSS STITCH with Back Stitch

To cover 1 square inch of fourteen mesh mono-canvas, it takes 6⅔ yards of Persian wool, single thread doubled over.

This stitch is almost the same as the previous stitch. You might call this one a tall cross stitch with a belt. If you require a very hard wearing, rough feeling stitch, here it is. It is sort of knotty looking, and is not at all apt to snag. This stitch is similar in appearance to the knotted stitch but they are constructed differently. This stitch is slow to work up, it does not pull the canvas out of shape and does have a very firm backing. Its major fault is that it is a wool-eater.

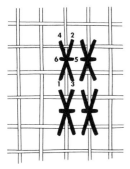

THE OBLONG CROSS STITCH WITH BACK STITCH

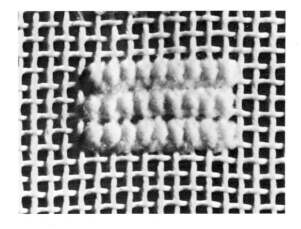

It takes 4⅓ yards of Persian wool, single thread doubled over,
to cover 1 square inch of fourteen mesh mono-canvas.

68

Stitches

The upright cross stitch gives a pin seal leather-like look, it is a tough stitch and hard to snag. It is useful for subject as well as background-ing. For a polka dot effect one could leave out a stitch here and there and then later fill it in with another color. It does require strong fingers to work. The upright cross stitch can be worked from right to left and then back from left to right. It is important with this stitch as with the previous cross stitch to make sure the crosses all cross in the same direction.

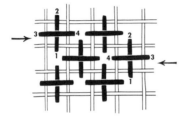

THE UPRIGHT CROSS STITCH

x *THE SMYRNA CROSS STITCH*

To cover 1 square inch of fourteen mesh mono-canvas, it takes
4 yards of Persian wool, single thread doubled over.

This is a very neat bulky stitch and is surprisingly unsnaggy. It works
equally well on both canvases and has a firm backing. Again you
must watch which way the crosses go.

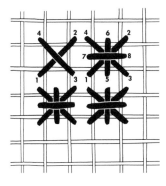

THE SMYRNA CROSS STITCH

THE DOUBLE CROSS STITCH

It takes 4 yards of Persian wool used full strand (all three threads at once)
to cover 1 square inch of fourteen mesh mono-canvas.

70

Stitches

The double cross stitch really could be called the two cross stitch. This would be a better description since this stitch is really a combination of the cross stitch and the upright cross stitch. The wool must fit the canvas exactly for this stitch, just fat enough, otherwise canvas will show through. The double cross stitch is attractive done in one color, it is also attractive with the cross stitch done in one color and the upright cross done in another color. Don't forget to watch the direction of your crosses.

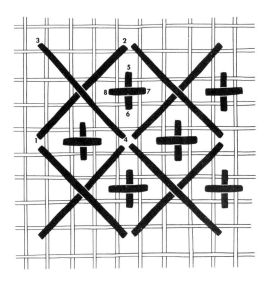

THE DOUBLE CROSS STITCH

It takes 4⅔ yards of Persian wool, single thread doubled over, to cover 1 square inch of fourteen mesh mono-canvas.

The double stitch is very like the double cross stitch in both name and the way it is done. The big difference is that the big cross stitch is a long cross stitch. The result is a neat woven effect. Watch your cross direction.

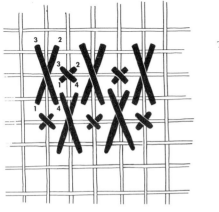

THE DOUBLE STITCH

XIII *THE RICE STITCH or the Crossed Corners Stitch or the William and Mary Stitch*

The rice stitch takes 2⅔ yards of Persian wool, single thread,
on fourteen mesh mono-canvas to cover 1 square inch.

The rice stitch is another one that must have the wool fitting exactly
if the stitch is to be effective at all. You must experiment until you are
satisfied that no canvas shows through the wool but that at the same
time the stitch does not look too crowded. A single thread of Persian
wool *not* doubled over works well on fourteen mesh mono-canvas and
a single thread of Persian wool doubled over works well for penelope
canvas ten mesh to the inch. The rice stitch is really just the cross stitch
with its arms tied down. Try doing the cross stitch in one color and
the tie-downs in another shade of the same color.

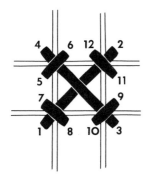

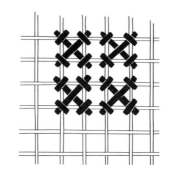

THE RICE STITCH

XIV *THE DOUBLE STRAIGHT CROSS STITCH*

It takes 3 yards of Persian wool used full strand to cover 1 square inch of fourteen mesh mono-canvas in the big crosses, and 1⅔ yards used single thread doubled over to do the little crosses.

This stitch is very similar to the upright cross stitch. The big difference is that the double straight cross stitch must be worked over four mesh each way and it has an extra cross to hold it down. It is very important to fit the wool to the canvas just so or the canvas will show through. Make sure all of your little crosses are going in the same direction.

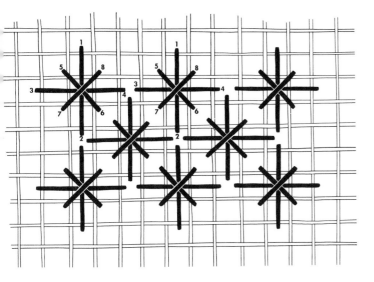

THE DOUBLE STRAIGHT CROSS STITCH

xv *THE DOUBLE LEVIATHAN STITCH*

It takes 3⅔ yards of Persian wool used single thread doubled over
to cover 1 square inch of fourteen mesh monocanvas.

74

Stitches

The double leviathan stitch may be used in rows or as a separate
decorative stitch. A single square of the stitch makes quite a high
bump on the canvas, very much like the popcorn stitch in crochet. If
necessary to cover the canvas a long upright stitch may be used between the squares of stitches. When designing the space for this stitch
make sure it is divisible by four since this stitch does not halve very
well.

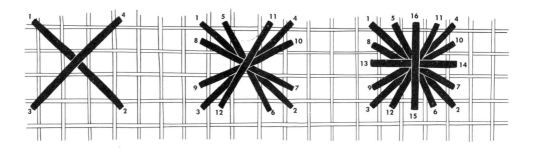

THE DOUBLE LEVIATHAN STITCH

THE TRIPLE LEVIATHAN STITCH

It takes 26 inches of Persian wool used single thread doubled over
to make just one triple leviathan on fourteen mesh mono-canvas.

The triple leviathan stitch is a decorative stitch to be used by itself. It
will not work up into horizontal or diagonal rows. It shows itself off
to best advantage on a fairly large mesh canvas. It also looks well in
two colors.

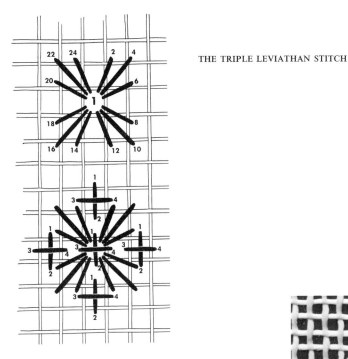

THE TRIPLE LEVIATHAN STITCH

On fourteen mesh mono-canvas it takes 2⅔ yards of Persian wool, single thread, to cover 1 square inch; on penelope ten mesh to the inch it takes 3⅔ yards of Persian wool using one thread doubled over.

76

Stitches

The star stitch can be done on both penelope and mono-canvas but it really looks better on the penelope. It makes a flat square pattern and is rather slow working up because you keep going back to the center mesh over and over. It must fit the canvas just right on either type otherwise canvas will show through. It has a reasonably firm backing.

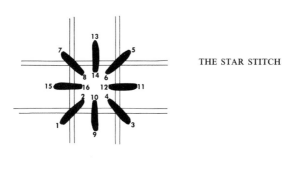

THE STAR STITCH

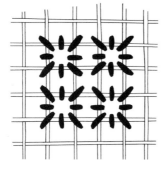

XVIII *THE DIAMOND EYELET STITCH*

To cover 1 square inch of fourteen mesh mono-canvas it takes
3⅔ yards of Persian wool used single thread doubled over.

The wool used with the diamond eyelet stitch must fit the canvas just
right because it must make so many passages through one canvas
mesh. If the wool is too thick you will not be able to complete the
stitch, and if it is too thin the outer edges of the canvas will show
through. A running stitch may be used to outline the diamonds.

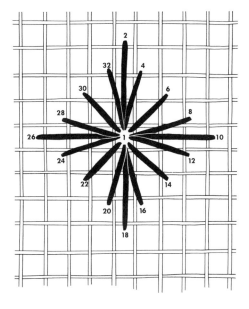

THE DIAMOND EYELET STITCH

XIX THE STRAIGHT GOBELIN STITCH or the Upright Gobelin Stitch and THE RENAISSANCE STITCH

To cover 1 square inch of fourteen mesh mono-canvas, it takes 3⅝ yards of Persian wool full strand, not doubled over, in the needle.

The Gobelin stitch is another of the very old stitches. There are several variations of it which follow. In order to keep canvas from peeking through, it is necessary to use the Persian wool full strand on most of the Gobelin type stitches. Try to keep the strand untwisted as you work, the stitch looks neater untwisted and the wool is fatter when lying straight.

You can tramé this stitch and then it is called the Renaissance stitch. The tramé will beef it up and give it a more pronounced ridge. Tramé unevenly over every other two horizontal threads on mono-canvas. If you are going to tramé on penelope canvas, bring the needle up between the woof threads, these are the two threads that are close together that one would ordinarily work over as one thread. Tramé over these threads. Do all the tramé, then the stitch.

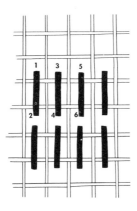

THE STRAIGHT GOBELIN STITCH

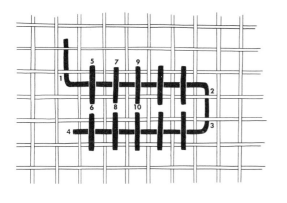

79

Stitches

xx   *THE SLANTING GOBELIN STITCH*

To cover 1 square inch of fourteen mesh mono-canvas, it takes 3⅓ yards of Persian wool used full strand.

The slanting Gobelin stitch is just like the upright except that it tilts. It covers the canvas more adequately than the upright. This stitch can be used over up to five horizontal threads or over two vertical threads as well as one. It has a very firm backing.

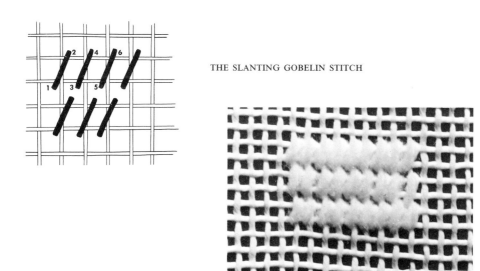

THE SLANTING GOBELIN STITCH

THE INTERLOCKING GOBELIN STITCH

or the Encroaching Gobelin Stitch

It takes 4⅓ yards of Persian wool, single thread doubled over,
to cover 1 square inch of fourteen mesh mono-canvas.

80

Stitches

This is a most attractive stitch, it works up quickly, makes a smooth hard surface on top and gives a thick backing. Its one drawback is that it pulls the canvas out of shape, but not too badly. It can be worked over just two threads of canvas or up to five, but you will have to fatten up your wool as your stitch gets longer.

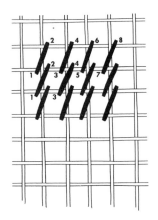

THE INTERLOCKING GOBELIN STITCH

Nelly Custis Lewis worked the firescreen which stands in the music room of her former home, Woodlawn Plantation, Mount Vernon, Virginia. The floral design was worked over canvas which was basted to wool broadcloth. Each stitch went through both canvas and cloth, upon completion the canvas threads were pulled out leaving the stitches on the broadcloth background.

XXII *THE ENCROACHING OBLIQUE STITCH*

It takes 3⅕ yards of Persian wool, single thread doubled over,
to cover 1 square inch of fourteen mesh mono-canvas.

82

Stitches

The encroaching oblique stitch is the interlocking or encroaching Gobelin stitch tilted over on its side. The two stitches could be combined on one canvas if you wanted your textures to go in two different directions. The encroaching oblique stitch makes a good background stitch, it has a nice smooth thickness on both sides of the canvas. It works up quickly and can be stitched in both directions, right to left and then left to right. This stitch uses less wool than the encroaching Gobelin and so is to be preferred to it.

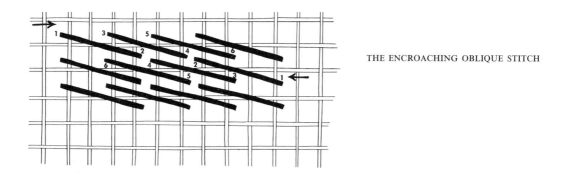

THE ENCROACHING OBLIQUE STITCH

To cover 1 square inch of fourteen mesh canvas,
it takes 3⅖ yards of Persian wool used full strand.

The plaited Gobelin has a rough woven look very well suited to today's modern interior decoration. It is a deceptive stitch in that it is
not as loose and snaggy as it looks. The only problem with this stitch
is having the wool fat enough to really cover the canvas. It works up
quickly and is rather fun to do.

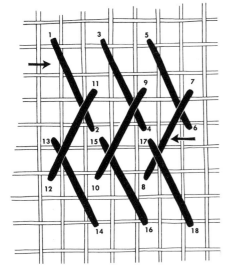

THE PLAITED GOBELIN STITCH

It takes 3½ yards of Persian wool used full strand to
cover 1 square inch of fourteen mesh mono-canvas.

84

Stitches

The brick or alternating stitch is a variation of the straight Gobelin
stitch. It is a good utility stitch, it is hard wearing and does not require too much thought to do. A full strand of Persian wool must be
used on this stitch, otherwise canvas will show through.

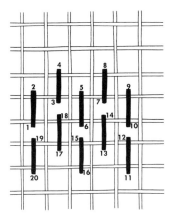

THE BRICK STITCH

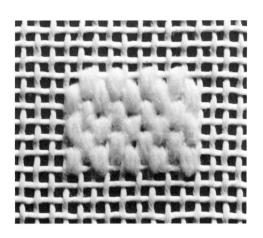

xxv *THE PARISIAN EMBROIDERY STITCH*

It takes 2⅔ yards of Persian wool full strand to cover 1 square inch of fourteen mesh canvas.

The next dozen stitches are variations on the same theme, long and short stitches in combination. Each combination makes its own special geometrical pattern. The Parisian embroidery stitch looks quite similar to the double stitch, but it is not a cross stitch. It forms a nice little pattern by itself or, if used in two colors, a sort of junior bargello pattern. It is very economical of wool. Most of these upright stitches require the use of the full strand of wool because otherwise the vertical thread of the canvas shows through.

85

Stitches

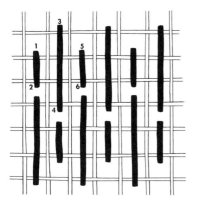

THE PARISIAN EMBROIDERY STITCH

It takes 2⅔ yards of Persian wool used full strand to
cover 1 square inch of fourteen mesh mono-canvas.

It is hard to tell the Parisian embroidery stitch from the Hungarian
embroidery stitch unless you remember that the Hungarian forms a
separate little square, whereas the Parisian is more of a stripe. This
stitch is pretty done in two colors, alternating the colors square by
square. It is a rather tricky stitch until you get the hang of it. Neither
this nor the Parisian embroidery stitch has much of a backing to it.

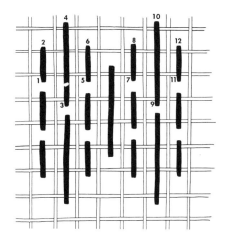

THE HUNGARIAN EMBROIDERY STITCH

Detail of curtains worked with Chinoiserie subjects. French, early 18th century.

XXVII *THE BARGELLO STITCH or the Florentine Stitch or the Flame Stitch*

It takes 2⅔ yards of Persian wool used full strand to cover 1 square inch of fourteen mesh mono-canvas.

The bargello stitch is the classic stitch done through all the periods of needlepoint history. Basically it is a straight Gobelin stitch worked over a random number of threads in a symmetrical pattern. It is not done in a straight line right across the canvas but should be done in peaks and valleys to form the "flames." When it is worked in various bright colors you can see why it is called the flame stitch. This is an interesting stitch to do and like all these big stitches quick to work up.

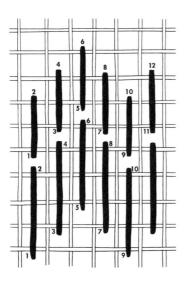

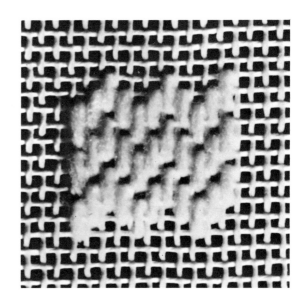

THE BARGELLO STITCH

Opposite: A bell pull showing an interesting use of the bargello stitch, probably made in the 18th century.

Doctor and Mrs. Henry L. Darner of Washington, D. C. worked on the needlepoint for this chair together; he did the traméed pattern, and she did the background. Especially made for the needlepoint, the chair is of applewood.

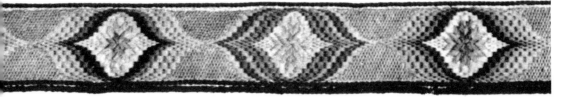

XXVIII *THE OLD FLORENTINE STITCH*

It takes 2⅔ yards of Persian wool used full strand
on fourteen mesh mono-canvas to cover 1 square inch.

A better name for this stitch would be the old Parisian stitch because
if you worked it over as few mesh as possible you would have a double
Parisian stitch. The smallest you can make the long part of this stitch
is over six threads of canvas. It is obviously not very snag-proof nor
does it have an evenly thick backing, but it does work up quickly and
is economical of wool.

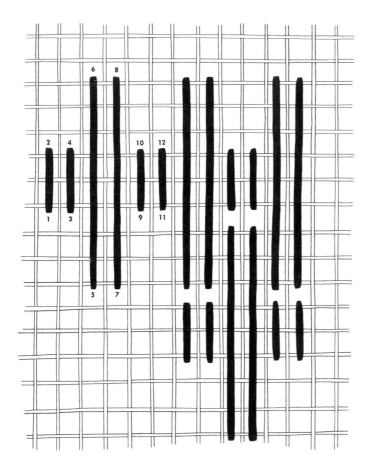

THE OLD FLORENTINE STITCH

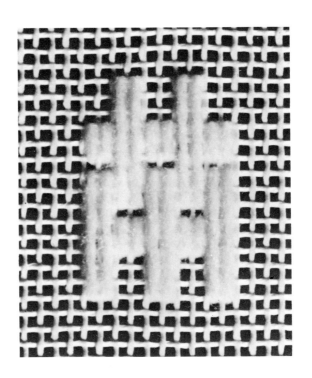

THE OLD FLORENTINE STITCH

XXIX *THE MOSAIC STITCH*

To cover 1 square inch of fourteen mesh mono-canvas, it takes 3⅓ yards of Persian wool, single thread doubled over.

The mosaic stitch and the following three stitches all respond nicely to being worked in two colors to form a checkerboard pattern. They all pull the canvas out of shape somewhat, so try not to do them tightly. This stitch has a firm backing. The mosaic stitch has a variation which is done diagonally and which forms a diagonally striped pattern. See also stitch number XXXIII.

THE MOSAIC STITCH

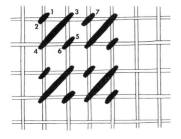

To cover 1 square inch of fourteen mesh mono-canvas, it takes
2⅔ yards of Persian wool, single thread doubled over.

As you can see, the Scotch stitch is an enlarged mosaic stitch. This stitch can be used in combination with other stitches to form very interesting patterns. For instance, the Scotch squares may be turned around to form a quarter square pattern bordered with half cross stitches. Alternating squares of half cross stitch with squares of Scotch stitch will form a checker-like pattern; it is sometimes called the checker stitch. Another variation to make the stitch a little more snag-proof is to weave the needle over and under the stitch to make a woven effect. You must remember to weave always in the same direction. Try using a weaving thread of a different color than the rest of the square itself.

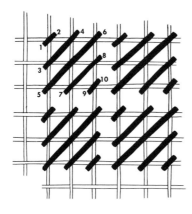

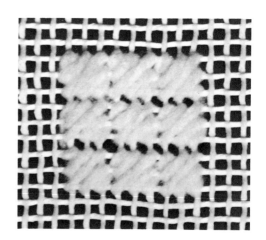

THE SCOTCH STITCH

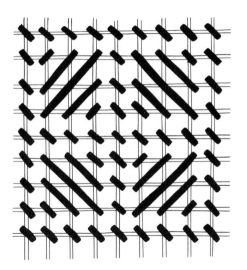

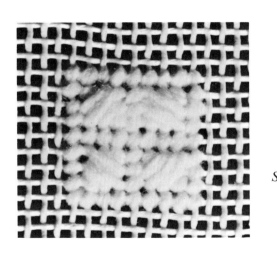

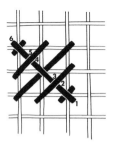

Variations on the Scotch stitch

THE CHECKER STITCH, a variation of the Scotch stitch

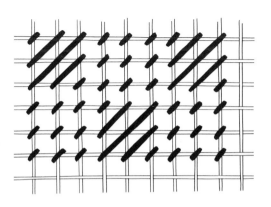

It takes just a couple of inches over 3 yards of Persian wool, single thread doubled over, to cover 1 square inch of fourteen mesh mono-canvas.

The cashmere stitch has a neat embossed look about it, more so than the other square or rectangular stitches. It also has a variation that is done diagonally.

THE CASHMERE STITCH

"Saint George and the Dragon," a wall hanging, measuring 3 by 8½ feet, worked in the mosaic stitch done diagonally (p. 96), the cashmere stitch done diagonally (p. 97) and up-side down, and the half cross stitch for the background. The background is grey, the subject green and yellow.

It takes 3½ yards of Persian wool used full strand to
cover 1 square inch of fourteen mesh mono-canvas.

The triangle stitch is a splashy geometric patterned stitch. It is not very
snag-proof but it does have a good firm backing.

95

Stitches

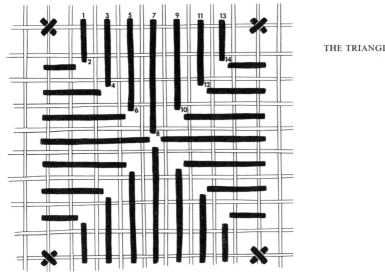

THE TRIANGLE STITCH

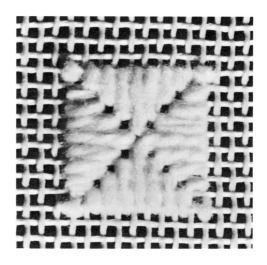

It takes exactly 3 yards of Persian wool, single thread doubled over,
to cover 1 square inch of fourteen mesh mono-canvas.

96

Stitches

This is one of five stitches which, using an oblique long stitch, form diagonal stripes. All of them have a good firm backing which assures better wear. The mosaic stitch done diagonally is quick and fun to do and is not too much of a wool-eater.

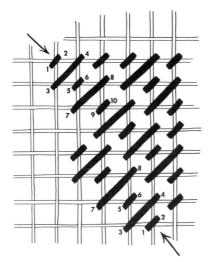

THE MOSAIC STITCH DONE DIAGONALLY

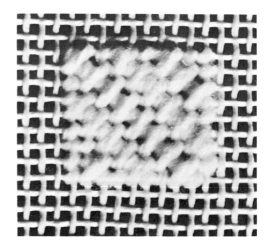

It takes 3⅖ yards of Persian wool, single thread doubled over, to cover 1 square inch of fourteen mesh mono-canvas.

This is a good tight stitch, it makes an excellent backgrounding because its pattern is not glaringly geometrical or distracting. Start it from the top of the canvas and work down or from left to right. Doing the cashmere stitch this way uses just a little more wool than the other way (XXXI).

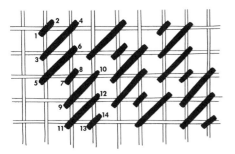

THE CASHMERE STITCH DONE DIAGONALLY

It takes 2⅝ yards of Persian wool, single thread doubled over,
to cover 1 square inch of fourteen mesh mono-canvas.

The Milanese stitch is not particularly snag-proof, and it does pull the canvas out of shape but it makes a pretty pattern and is quite economical of wool.

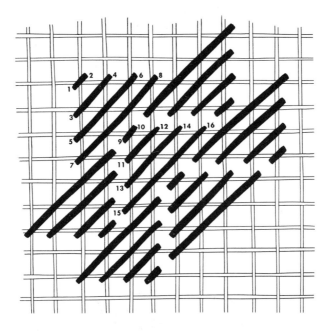

THE MILANESE STITCH

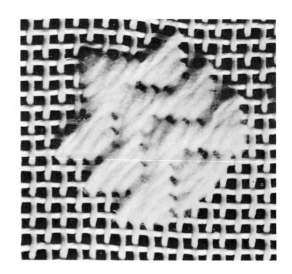

It takes exactly 3 yards of Persian wool, single thread doubled over, to cover 1 square inch of fourteen mesh mono-canvas.

The Byzantine stitch is fairly easy to do once the first zigzag stripe is done from top to bottom. You just follow the steps it made. The simplest way to do the stitch is from left to right. It does not pull the canvas out of shape as much as the others. Try it in very strong colors.

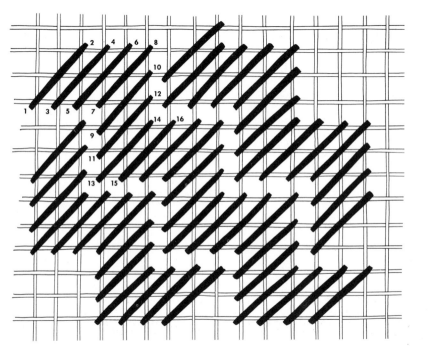

THE BYZANTINE STITCH

"The Queen of Sheba Admiring the Wisdom of Solomon" is the title of the petit point picture which was made in Massachusetts in 1744. Note the fiddler on the right of the tent and the man with his tankard of ale on the left.

XXXVII *THE SCOTCH STITCH DONE DIAGONALLY* or *THE DIAGONAL STITCH*

To cover 1 square inch of fourteen mesh mono-canvas, it takes 3 yards and 3 inches of Persian wool, single thread doubled over.

This stitch is perhaps a little more interesting to look at than the Byzantine stitch and it uses just a little more wool. It fits into smaller spaces possibly because it does not lead the eye as strongly or because the "steps" are shorter.

THE SCOTCH STITCH
DONE DIAGONALLY

To cover 1 square inch of fourteen mesh mono-canvas, it takes
4½ yards of Persian wool, single thread doubled over.

The knotted stitch is the first of three tie-down stitches which are worked similarly though the results are different in appearance. You might call the knotted stitch a single tie-down, the French stitch a double tie-down, and the rococo stitch a quadruple tie-down. They are all basically a long stitch with a catch stitch in the middle.

The knotted stitch has been mentioned before in connection with the oblong cross stitch with back-stitch (VIII). The knotted stitch takes strong hands to work, but it makes a tight snag-proof surface. It can be done in two strokes of the needle without having to put your hand under the canvas. It is done from right to left and does not pull the canvas out of shape if it is not done too tightly.

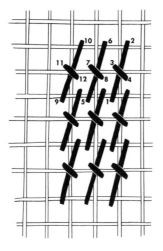

THE KNOTTED STITCH

The French stitch takes 3⅔ yards of Persian wool, single thread doubled over, to cover 1 square inch of fourteen mesh mono-canvas.

The French stitch is the double tie-down stitch. It is a hard tight stitch and quite snag-proof. For a mass effect the French stitch looks neater than the rococo stitch. It works up slowly but does not pull the canvas out of shape. It has a firm backing.

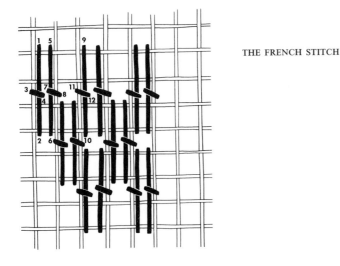

THE FRENCH STITCH

XL *THE ROCOCO STITCH*

It takes 5½ yards of Persian wool, single thread doubled over,
to cover 1 square inch of fourteen mesh mono-canvas.

The rococo stitch is the largest of the tie-down stitches. It is worked in diagonal rows. It can be used singly as a diagonal stripe or in rows as a backgrounding. It looks very Victorian when done in mass. This stitch is a terrible wool-eater.

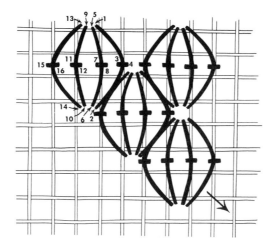

THE ROCOCO STITCH

It takes 3 yards of Persian wool, single thread, on fourteen mesh mono-canvas to cover 1 square inch.

The web stitch is a tie-down stitch at its most tied-down. In crewel embroidery it could be compared to couching. It is best described as tramé done diagonally. The result does not look like needlepoint, it has a more woven appearance, very close and hard. The backing is quite solid too. It is advisable to do this stitch on a fairly large mesh canvas for the sake of your eyesight. It works up very slowly, it would never do as a background stitch because it is so tedious. It is mainly a special effects or accent stitch. Work the diagonal tramé stitches first, then do the couching or tie-down stitches. Hold the canvas so that the web or tramé stitches are parallel to your body, you can follow the tie-down stitch placement better that way.

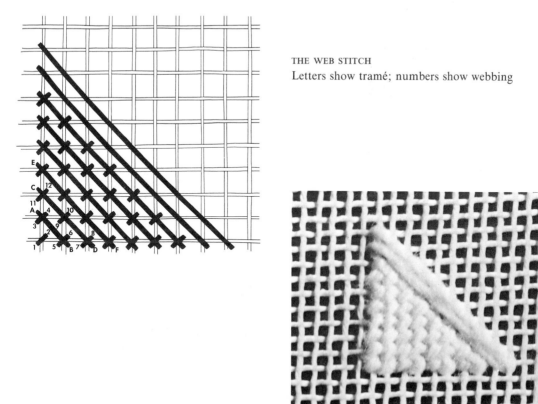

THE WEB STITCH
Letters show tramé; numbers show webbing

THE CHAIN STITCH

To cover 1 square inch of fourteen mesh mono-canvas,
it takes 2⅓ yards of Persian wool, single thread.

The chain stitch does not look like needlepoint, it looks like knitting. Each stitch ties down the stitch before it. It takes some experimenting to get the wool to fit the canvas exactly, the problem being to have the wool thin enough not to crowd the mesh together as the stitch is worked. At the same time the wool must be fat enough to cover the canvas. Penelope canvas accommodates this stitch better than mono-canvas. The chain stitch is worked from top to bottom only. Include the loop of the last stitch worked on each new stitch. Loop the wool under the needle to form the next stitch.

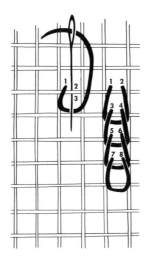

THE CHAIN STITCH

XLIII   *THE KNITTING STITCH*

It takes 4⅙ yards of Persian wool, single thread doubled over, to cover 1 square inch of fourteen mesh mono-canvas.

The following ten stitches all form braids or stripes of stitching. They are formed by different arrangements or crossings of obliquely made long stitches.

The knitting stitch makes a very nice background stitch. This stitch and the one following are almost identical except that one stripes horizontally and the other vertically. Both stitches look very much like knitting and are handsome used on the same canvas together. The little bare space at the end of each row must be filled in with a half cross stitch. The knitting stitch is rather tiresome to do because there is no quick way to work it without wasting wool and spreading canvas threads into each other. The temptation is to do it like a giant continental stitch, but you must push the needle through the canvas and then reach for it on the under side every stitch.

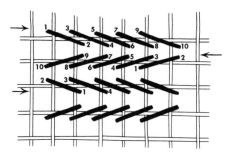

THE KNITTING STITCH

An eighteenth century wing chair; the covering is unusual in that though the pattern is a typical bargello one, the stitch is the kalem stitch.

THE KALEM STITCH or the Reverse Tent Stitch

To cover 1 square inch of fourteen mesh mono-canvas, it takes 4⅙ yards of Persian wool, used single thread doubled over.

This is the other stitch of the knitting pair. It is worked vertically rather than horizontally. You may find it easier, however, to hold the canvas as you would for the knitting stitch. The kalem and the knitting stitch take the same amount of wool. When used on rugs the kalem stitch is sometimes called the tapestry stitch.

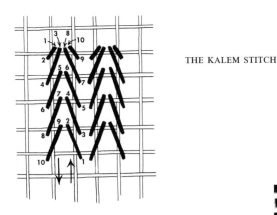

THE KALEM STITCH

XLV   *THE HERRINGBONE STITCH or the Plaited Stitch and THE HERRINGBONE STITCH GONE WRONG*

The herringbone stitch takes 4½ yards of Persian wool, single thread doubled over, to cover 1 square inch of fourteen mesh mono-canvas. The amount is the same for the herringbone gone wrong.

The herringbone stitch presents a rather tweedy finished surface. It is a hard, slow-moving stitch to do on fine canvas, not recommended for great expanses of background. However, on a large mesh canvas it moves right along. On rug canvas it is a great over-all stitch. It must be done from left to right *only,* not back and forth, or you will not produce the herringbone pattern. You must do a row and then finish off the thread, go back to the left side and start all over again.

But perhaps you'll like the herringbone gone wrong pattern more. It is produced by going from left to right and then back again, *right* to *left.* The result is a pretty weave on the bias. This stitch is also done on the larger mesh canvas because it is easier to get the needle down between the stitches already done. Neither stitch has much on the reverse side.

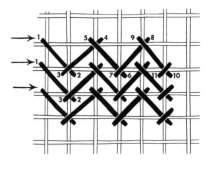

THE HERRINGBONE STITCH

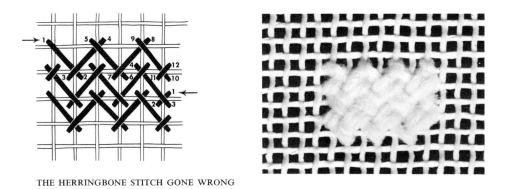

THE HERRINGBONE STITCH GONE WRONG

XLVI *THE TWO-COLOR HERRINGBONE STITCH*

It takes 3⅔ yards of Persian wool (both colors), single thread doubled over, to cover 1 square inch of fourteen mesh mono-canvas.

This stitch is primarily a rug stitch but it also works well on finer mesh canvas as a separate stripe or just in rows. The foundation stitches are done in one color and then the top stitches are done over them in another color. Of course, it can be worked in one solid color.

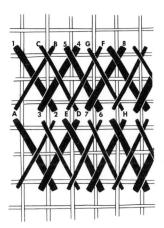

THE TWO-COLOR HERRINGBONE STITCH
Letters show one color; numbers show the other color

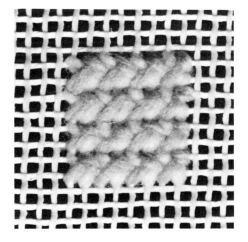

To cover 1 square inch of fourteen mesh mono-canvas, it
takes only 1 yard of Persian wool used full strand.

112

Stitches

The oblique Slav stitch is worked diagonally. It is rather difficult to
understand at first but quite simple to do, once you catch on. It
works best with a fat wool on a finer mesh canvas so the canvas will
not show through. It covers a lot of ground quickly and is very
economical of wool. Its faults are that it is not very snag-proof, nor
does it have much of a backing for long-wear insurance. It may also
be worked horizontally, as shown in the second diagram.

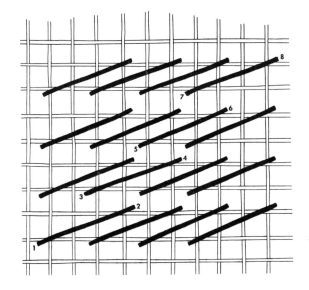

THE OBLIQUE SLAV STITCH,
done diagonally

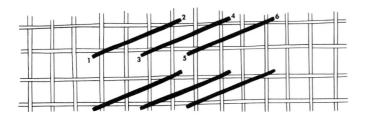

THE OBLIQUE SLAV STITCH,
done horizontally

XLVIII   *THE FERN STITCH*

To cover 1 square inch of fourteen mesh mono-canvas, it takes
3⅗ yards of Persian wool, single thread doubled over.

The fern stitch makes a fat neat braid, it looks similar to a very thick
wale corduroy. It is quick and easy to work up and has a nice thick
backing. It must be worked from top to bottom only.

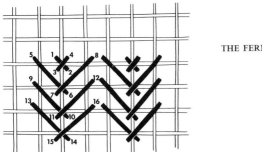

THE FERN STITCH

It takes 3⅓ yards of Persian wool, single thread doubled over,
to cover 1 square inch of fourteen mesh mono-canvas.

114

Stitches

This stitch is very similar to the previous one except that it looks a little lop-sided. It is just as attractive and as easy to do. Try doing the long stitch in one color and the short stitch in another color. In working the stitch one does all the long stitches first and then all of the short stitches.

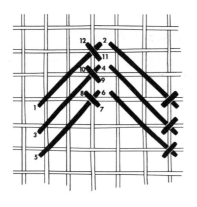

THE LONG AND SHORT OBLIQUE STITCH

An antique child's chair with oyster pattern covering.

L THE STEM STITCH *or the Long Oblique Stitch*
with Running Stitch and THE PERSPECTIVE STITCH

The total amount of wool used for the long oblique stitch with running stitch comes to 3 yards and 3 inches of Persian wool on fourteen mesh mono-canvas covering 1 square inch. The perspective stitch takes 1⅝ yards of Persian wool (this includes both colors) used full strand to cover 1 square inch of fourteen mesh mono-canvas.

The stem stitch is another cordurory-like stitch, simple to do and with a nice fat backing. It can be done in two colors by working the oblique stitches in one color and the running stitches in the other. Use half

THE STEM STITCH

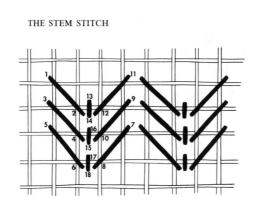

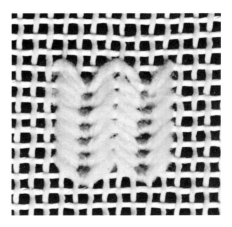

THE PERSPECTIVE STITCH

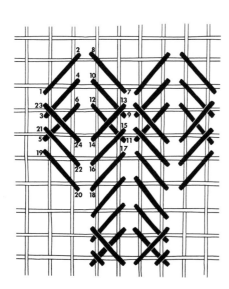

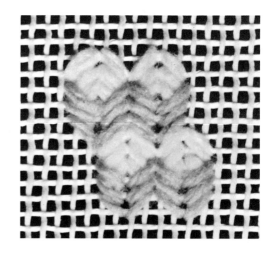

the weight wool in the running stitch that you did for the oblique. For instance, a single thread doubled over for the oblique stitch, and for the running stitch the same wool used singly in the needle.

The perspective stitch does not use the running stitch, just three pairs of oblique stitches overlapping three more pairs of oblique stitches heading in the opposite direction. This stitch can be done in one color, but one color does not do it justice, one needs two colors to show the "box" illusion of the stitch. The wool must fit the canvas on this stitch otherwise the center will show canvas.

LI   *THE GREEK STITCH or the Double Back Stitch or the Long-armed Cross Stitch*

It takes 3⅓ yards of Persian wool, single thread doubled over, to cover 1 square inch of fourteen mesh mono-canvas.

The Greek stitch is a combination of the cross stitch and a braid stitch. It has a busier look than the previous braid stitches and really looks as though it had been plaited. It does not have much of a backing but it is quite snag-proof. The railway stitch following is a more complex version of this one. The Greek stitch is often used as a rug stitch.

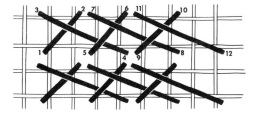

THE GREEK STITCH

The larger figures are worked with silk on canvas and applied to a white satin ground worked with metal threads. English mid-17th century.

It takes just 3 yards of Persian wool, single thread doubled over, to cover 1 square inch of fourteen mesh mono-canvas.

Why this stitch is named either knit or railway is hard to understand. It does not look like knitting nor does it look like railway tracks. It makes a fat braid when worked up. It would work well as a heavy stripe. It is very hard on the eyes and requires one's constant attention. It covers the canvas very well but is quite snaggy. More canvas threads are covered in this stitch than in the Greek stitch which is its simpler version, and weaving is involved in this stitch and not in the Greek. Work all the left to right stitches at once, then come back along the same row working the right to left stitches. You will weave under the last two wool threads before your needle goes back into the canvas as shown in the diagram.

119

Stitches

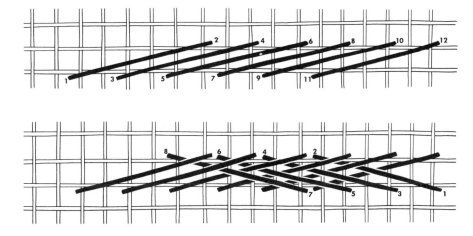

THE RAILWAY STITCH

It takes 3¼ yards of Persian wool, single thread doubled over,
to cover 1 square inch of fourteen mesh mono-canvas.

120

Stitches

The leaf stitch is one of the most attractive and unusual of the fancy stitches. It is not particularly hard to do, has a nice backing and does not use an inordinate amount of wool. Its only drawback is that it is not very snag-proof. This stitch can be made smaller by reducing the number of mesh covered overall and dropping a pair of "veins" entirely. An upright stitch can be inserted on the leaf to resemble the main stem if desired.

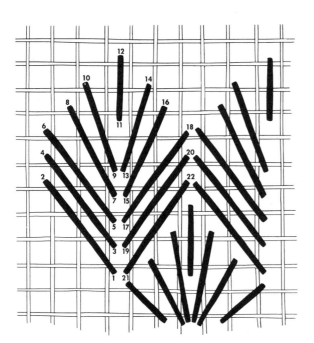

THE LEAF STITCH

It takes 5 yards of Persian wool, single thread doubled over,
to cover 1 square inch of fourteen mesh mono-canvas.

The darning stitch is basically a rug stitch but it is rather hard to do
with real rug wool on rug canvas. It fits a large mesh mono-canvas
using tapestry wool much better. Persian wool used full strand is
satisfactory too. It is a great wool-eater but it is geared for very
heavy wear. Of course, it won't last if your cat sharpens his claws on
it. The stitch is worked in four journeys over the same set of holes.
Go over four canvas threads and under two to the edge. On the
return trip you will go over the threads you went under the last time,
and under the threads you went over. Make these journeys back and
forth once more, then the stitch is completed.

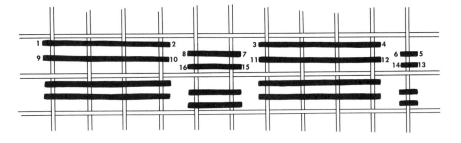

THE DARNING STITCH

LV *THE SURREY STITCH*

It takes 7⅔ yards to cover 1 square inch of fourteen mesh mono-canvas.

The surrey stitch is the simplest of the loop stitches. There are other loop stitches but they are so tricky to do and so elaborate when worked up they seem to belong in needle-made lace rather than needlepoint. The surrey stitch is a rug stitch, but figures are given on fourteen mesh mono-canvas to show the relative amount of wool that would be needed on rug canvas. This makes a nice fluffy pile. The stitch works up quickly and does not stretch the canvas out of shape.

If the stitch is done on mono-canvas, two canvas threads each way should be used. Real rug canvas or a large mesh penelope is to be preferred. It takes a little time to catch on to this stitch. It is started at the bottom and worked up the canvas row by row. You can use your left thumb as your loop or pile gauge. After each row is completed the loops should be cut before you start the next row. Three quarters of an inch (uncut) is a good amount to use as your pile gauge.

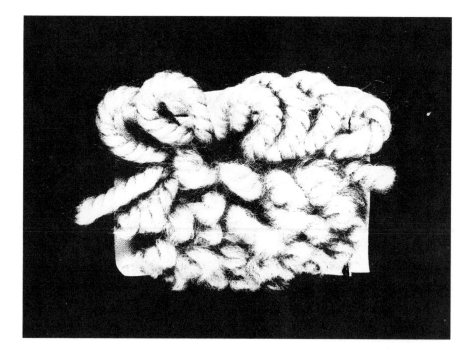

To start the stitch bring the needle in and out of the canvas as in diagram a. Holding down with your thumb the tag of wool left out, bring the needle and wool around to the left and insert it from the right in the space next door as in diagrams b and c. The needle must pass over its own tail, so to speak, to form the knot. Pull the wool tight and the knot is secure. To start the next stitch insert the needle at X as in diagram d. To start the next row begin on the row just above the row completed.

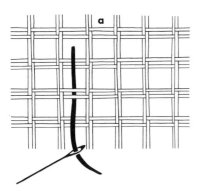

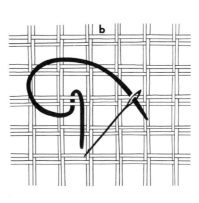

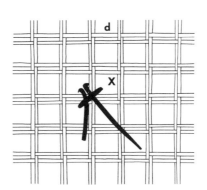

THE SURREY STITCH

The King Charles Spaniel with his bright glass eyes was worked in the surrey stitch around 1870. The contours of his body were skillfully clipped in. The dog sits on a silk cross stitch cushion with beaded trim.

RUGS

Rugs lend themselves to the use of fancy stitches particularly well. The stitches most commonly used are the single cross stitch, the double cross stitch, the rice stitch, the Greek stitch, both herringbone stitches, the knitting stitch, the darning stitch, and the surrey stitch. The rug stitches were tested on five mesh to the inch rug canvas with regular rug wool. Some were done by the square inch and some by two square inches because the stitches are so big that they could not be completed on just one inch full of mesh. To figure out what yardage of wool one square inch would take just divide the yardage of the two square inches by four.

Rug wool is sold by the pound. It is used on eight mesh canvas and on down to three mesh. Tapestry wool used double thread or full strands of Persian wool are used for rugs done on mono-canvas ten mesh to the inch. See the section on wool for more information on rug wool.

THE RUG STITCHES

The single cross stitch makes a neat rug stitch, not shaggy and with a good backing. It is used in rug making to define the design. Using rug wool on five mesh to the inch rug canvas it takes 25 inches of wool to cover 1 square inch.

The double cross stitch is not as snag-free nor does it have as firm a backing as the single cross stitch. It takes 2½ yards of rug wool to cover 2 square inches of five mesh rug canvas.

The rice stitch makes a nondescript pattern when done on rug canvas. It has a firm backing. To cover 2 square inches of five mesh rug canvas it takes 3⅓ yards of rug wool.

The Greek stitch makes a big fat braid if you use the wool double in the needle. It is too thin if used singly, canvas shows through. If you want all of the braids to point in the same direction do the stitch only from left to right. A little filling-in has to be done at the beginning of each row because the first stitch lacks its long arm. It takes 3⅔ yards of rug wool used doubled in the needle to cover 2 square inches of five mesh rug canvas.

The surrey stitch is mainly a rug stitch, it can be used in combination with other stitches or by itself. It takes close to 2 yards of rug wool to cover 1 square inch of five mesh rug canvas.

The herringbone stitch done correctly or "incorrectly" is a superior rug stitch. Both are tight, pretty and economical of wool. It takes 2 yards and 3 inches of rug wool to cover 2 square inches of five mesh rug canvas.

The two-color herringbone is another fine rug stitch, particularly if you want a tweedy effect. It takes 2 yards and 8 inches of rug wool to cover 2 square inches of five mesh rug canvas.

The knitting stitch is rather monotonous to do but it is a good serviceable stitch. It can be used to work out designs. It takes 2 yards and 7 inches of rug wool to cover 2 square inches of five mesh rug canvas.

The darning stitch has a very homespun look. As mentioned before, this stitch works best when tapestry wool or Persian wool are used on a smaller meshed canvas. Rug wool is too hard and compressed a wool for this stitch, a springier wool is needed. It takes 3 yards of rug wool to cover 2 square inches of five mesh rug canvas.

Most rugs have a non-skid material stitched to the back when finished. Rugs that are seamed either have tape sewn on over the seam and/or a heavy muslin lining. On single strip rugs a binding stitch is worked over the selvages, fringe is looped over the ends and nothing more is done. Some rug makers do not line their rugs because they say that little stones and sand will work their way through the rug or the lining, be trapped and stay inside the rug to cut the wool over the years.

HOW TO BEGIN AND FINISH RUGS

To start a rug on rug canvas (a strip rug) or to start the outside edges of a seamed rug, fold back about two inches of canvas on the cut ends and match up the mesh. Using carpet thread sew the fold back as if it were a hem. Then work your stitches over the fold back as though it were just one layer of canvas instead of two. Do the same thing as you work toward the other cut end. Start your stitches just as you do on smaller mesh, by running your wool in and out of the can-

An inexpensive rug-hooking frame being used as a needlepoint rug frame; the stitch being used is the herringbone stitch gone wrong.

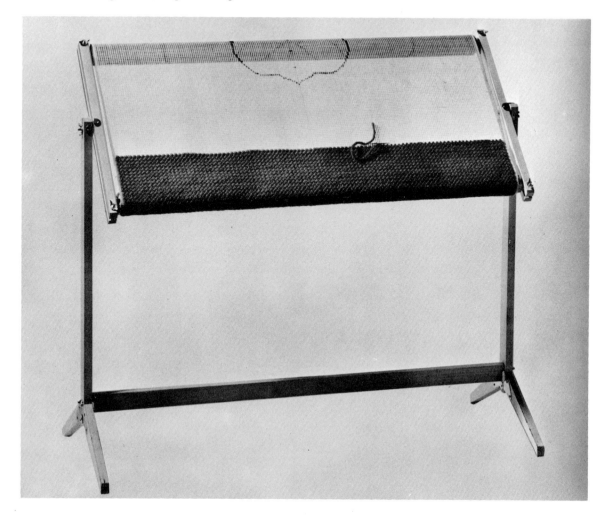

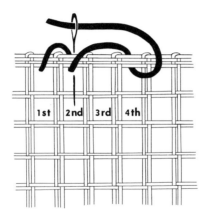

1st | 2nd | 3rd | 4th

vas and then stitching over that place to lash the end down. Be sure that your stitches are really secured at the end of a thread.

When doing a strip rug on rug canvas a frame is almost a necessity. The canvas is so heavy and stiff, your holding hand just will not be able to manage it after you have done a few inches. Speaking of hands, some rug canvas is so starchy it abrades your skin. Try clipping the finger tips out of an old soft cotton glove and see if that will help any.

The binding stitch that you will use on the selvages of strip rugs is best not diagramed. With the wrong side of the canvas facing you, work a stitch away from you and over the edge of the canvas and into the following hole. Skipping the next hole, go over the edge again and in through the back of the fourth hole. Now you reverse direction and go over the edge into the back of the second hole, reverse again and into the back of the fifth hole, reverse and into the back of the third hole. All of these stitches are made over the selvage, you understand. It sounds very confusing but is quite simple once you actually do it.

To make fringe for the ends of the strip rug cut the wool into six-inch pieces. With a crochet hook inserted through the canvas at the bottom row of mesh, catch the middle of the six-inch piece, pull it through the canvas far enough to make a loop through which you pull the ends (which are hanging from the other side of the canvas).

Pull the ends tight. Trim the fringe to even it off when you have finished.

A strip rug can be blocked just like a seat cover or any other piece of needlepoint. One needs an old door or a floor on which you don't mind making a few tack holes. Lay down a layer of brown paper, dampen the rug, lay it on the brown paper and stretch as you would that smaller canvas. Obviously, this is a two-man job. Actually you will find that there is very little stretching to do, especially if the rug was worked in a frame.

To piece together a seamed rug is a tiresome business. First machine stitch the finished pieces about one-third of an inch away from the worked canvas before you even start to join them. Each mesh and stitch must then be matched up with the corresponding stitch and mesh on the piece you wish to join. Baste the pieces together. The two pieces may be machine stitched together, using a loose stitch count, or they may be sewn together by hand. If you machine stitch them together you must try to stitch as close as you can to the center of the thread right next to the worked part. The corners are particularly hard to do because they must be mitred. Trim some of the excess canvas on the seam, press it flat, and sew tape over the seam by hand to insure that too much stress will not be put on the seam. Rug canvas does not piece at all well. There is a beautiful example of a pieced contemporary needlepoint rug on the floor of the sanctuary in the National Cathedral in Washington, D. C. It was worked on a smaller mesh canvas.

A book, *Reliquae Sacre Carolinae,* bound in petit point embroidery, English c. 1651.

New York Sky Line, pole screen
worked in petit point

A vest with hobby motifs

FINISHING YOUR CANVAS

When your piece is all finished and the tags and snips have been trimmed from the back, you are ready to stretch the canvas. The equipment you will need for the job is a box of aluminum tacks, or copper will do, a tack hammer, some brown paper, and a piece of wood larger than your canvas. This last could be an old drawing board or bread board, something on which you don't mind having tack holes. Tack the brown paper to the board, and in pencil draw an outline of the desired shape of the finished canvas. Dampen the canvas with a sponge or sprinkle it with cold water until it is quite damp all over. Lay it face down on the brown paper and see how it conforms to the desired outline. Then pull it and stretch it until it does conform, more or less.

Tack down the four corners about a half inch away from the finished work. Then with an even tension tack between each corner and so on quartering and re-quartering around the canvas, tugging every now and then to make the canvas fit the outline, until there is a tack about every inch all the way around. When blocking a circular shaped canvas, treat it as though it were a square as far as tacking is concerned but make it come true to its circular outline. The canvas should take about two days to dry.

Don't be tempted to use a stapling gun or stapler instead of the tacks. The staples will split and cut through the canvas threads just like a knife. It is almost impossible to remove the canvas from the board without a knife to pry up the staples, a very trying job.

A small stitch sampler stretched. Only the right half of the canvas was rabbit-skinned to show by contrast the thin coating required.

When your canvas is dry it is ready for its coating of rabbit skin glue, which must be applied while the canvas is still on the blocking board. Rabbit skin is usually used for sizing canvas of the oil painting variety. It is recommended for the back of any canvas that you think will slip back into its unstretched shape from wear. Under this heading would come pillows (just a thin coating), and handbags. It is a good idea to rabbit-skin the backs of pictures too. The purpose of rabbit skin glue is to keep the canvas blocked, to keep the canvas from losing its shape from use. A tin of rabbit skin may be purchased for about a dollar from an art supply store.

The proportions of water and glue are one ounce of the dry glue to a cup of water. Soak the glue in an unbreakable container for about an hour. It will then have softened and be ready for cooking. Place the container in a pan of cold water and heat it slowly, but not to the boiling point. Stir until smooth. It will be the consistency of pea soup. Remove the container from the hot water and set it aside to cool. When the gel is completely cool it will be the consistency of jello. Spread it with a knife all over the back of the canvas, but not so much that it will soak through to the front. Gently scrape off any excess. Be sure the area is covered completely. Then set your blocking board aside again to let the glue dry on the canvas. When the canvas is dry it will be quite stiff. Unless you plan to do another canvas within a week you may as well throw the rest of the cooked gel away, it does not keep very long.

MOUNTING

There are few things that you cannot mount yourself. Large upholstered furniture, chair backs and arms, and leather trimmed handbags are, of course, best done by professionals. Pillows, stools, slip seats, clutch bags, kneelers and pictures can be done at home. The most obvious advantage is economic. It costs from fifteen to thirty dollars to have a handbag finished professionally, sometimes more.

Slip Seats   When your seat cover is finished and stretched you should have an inch to a half inch more finished work all the way around the seat than you need. Place the canvas just the way you want it on the chair seat and stab through it with straight pins in the four corners and the center. This will help hold it in place while you are working on the back. Gently turn the canvas and seat over, bottom side up. With someone helping you, pull the canvas tight front and back and tack it. The tacks should go one half inch in from the edge. Pull the canvas tight from side to side and tack it. Fold the excess canvas over in the corners, pull it firmly and tack it by opposing corners. That is, tack one corner, then the one opposite, then the last two. If there is a lot of curve to the seat you will have to take little tucks in the canvas as you work around. Work your way around the canvas from side to side stretching *evenly* as you go. Turn the whole thing over occasionally to make sure you are not stretching unevenly. When you are finished you should have a tack about every inch or so. Trim the ruffle of canvas left, one-half inch from the tacks will do. Cover the bottom of the seat with black or white muslin using fewer tacks and placing them closer to the edge of the seat. Stretch the muslin taut, but not tight.

Pillows   Pillows look best with some cording or fringe at the edge. Commercial fringe looks very nice if you can match the color. You can make your own cording by cutting enough bias to go around the pillow from the material you are using to cover the back of the pillow. Fold the bias over common household cord and sew it as close as the sewing machine foot will allow. Sew your cording, cord side in, raw edge side out, on to the very edge of your finished canvas. Shaping is required when turning corners with the cording. Baste the pillow backing (right sides facing each other with the cording coming in be-tween) right along the seam of the cording. Machine stitch the canvas, cording and backing together, following the basting stitches and leav-ing an end open to reverse the cover and to insert the pillow. Hand

A true bargello chair seat, one of a set.

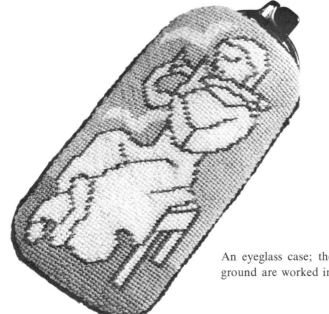

An eyeglass case; the lute player and the background are worked in four shades of blue.

A bargello purse on nylon net worked by a geriatric patient at a nursing home.

A cushion cover worked in wool, "The Prodigal Son Leaving His Parents," English early 17th century.

stitch the opening together as close to the cording seam as possible. The fringe can be handled the same way as the cording, the fringe will be facing in when you attach it to the worked canvas. Don't forget to shape the corners a little with the fringe too.

Clutch Bag   Do a piece of needlepoint 20 inches by 8 inches. (Your sampler?) When it is stretched and *lightly* rabbit-skinned, cut a piece of lining material an inch larger all around than your worked piece. Mount a zipper to the narrow ends of the needlepoint piece so that you have a large ring or muff of needlepoint and zipper. With the wrong side out sew the lengthwise seams of the needlepoint. The zipper will be in the middle of the purse, giving a saddle-bag-like pocket on each side of the zipper. Sew the seam right on the edge of the last worked stitch. Trim off the excess canvas within a half inch of the seam, trim the corners of excess bulk. Turn it right side out through the zipper opening.

Again with the wrong side out sew the sides of the lining material

A Victorian cricket stool with the diaper pattern covering is one of a pair; they were made from the tops of piano stools and the remains of the screw is still in the under side of each stool.

together so that you have a saddle-bag arrangement with a half inch of material separating each bag. Trim the seams of the lining and insert into the needlepoint envelope just the way it is. Stitch the lining to the zipper seam by hand on each side, and stitch the edges of the center of the lining to the zipper ends. Press with a damp cloth.

Footstools   The important thing with footstools is to make sure the finished work really fits the stool. Assuming that your stool cover has boxed corners, trim the excess canvas to within an inch all around and to within a half inch in the corners. Hem up the bare canvas to the back of the canvas with a basting stitch. Bring the corners together, then you can oversew them together with matching wool from the outside, or you can machine a seam from the wrong side. Oversewing from the outside insures that no bare canvas will shine through. Trim the corners of excess bulk. With upholstery tacks nail the needlepoint to the stool (with or without gimp). This is a two-man job, you will need someone to hold it in place as you work back and forth and from side to side.

Mounting a Picture   Stretch your canvas as true as you can and put on a good coating of rabbit skin glue. Cut a piece of cardboard one stitch smaller than your finished picture. The cardboard used in gift boxes is an excellent weight to use. Trim the excess canvas from your picture, leaving a generous inch on all sides and a generous half inch on the corners. With carpet thread and needle handy, fold back that half inch of bare canvas right to the corner stitch. Sew the folded edges together. Do this to the opposite corner next, and then the remaining two corners.

   If the picture is more than six inches across, lace the sides to each other with the carpet thread. Press each corner on the wrong side as hard as you can. You want the back of the picture to take up as little room as possible in the frame. If you are not having a framer go on from there, order a frame the exact measurement of your mounted

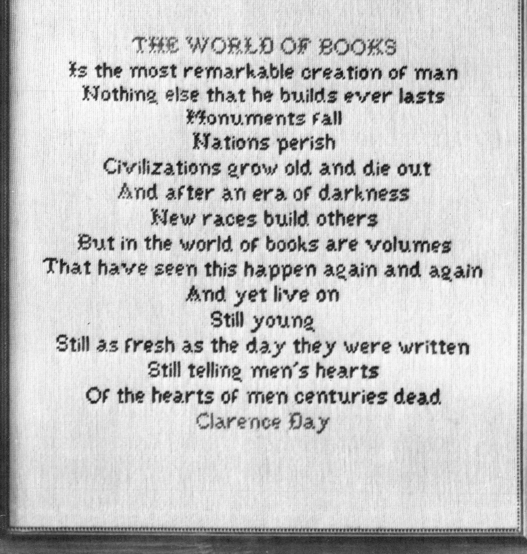

A quotation for a library; the frame, the title, and the name are in a warm rose color, the rest is in black and white.

In 1850 Mrs. Nelly Custis Lewis worked a silk bouclé bouquet of roses on perforated cardboard for her friend, Mrs. Oliver. The picture now hangs in the upstairs hall, Woodlawn Plantation, Mount Vernon.

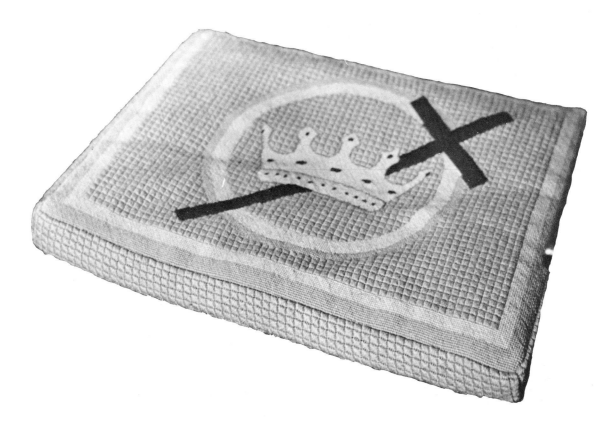

A cushion from the Resurrection Chapel of the National Cathedral, Washington, D. C. The background color of the cushions and kneelers in this chapel is aqua, the background stitch is the Scotch stitch.

canvas. Try to choose one that will be deep enough to hold the bulk. Vacuum-clean the canvas before you lay it in the frame, lay a piece of cardboard in on top and tack it with the nails provided, first in the center of each side and then a few nails close to the corners. Cut out a piece of brown paper just a quarter of an inch smaller than the frame edge. Glue this with a good stout glue to the back of the cardboard and the back edge of the frame. This paper cover will keep the dust out.

ET CETERA

Picking Out Mistakes   You need two things to pick out mistakes, a pair of sharp-nosed sewing scissors and a very light touch. Insert the tip of the scissor under the wool a stitch at a time, take it slow and easy, so as not to cut the canvas. Snip in the direction that you stitched. When you have snipped all the stitches that you need to, put away the scissors and pick out the stitches with a needle until you have reached the end of that thread or have enough to put in the needle to finish off in the back of the canvas. You will have to snip both front and back and then pick out your "snippage" with your fingernails. It is slow, delicate work but worth it to get rid of a mistake.

Joining Two Pieces of Canvas   Joining two pieces of bare canvas is considerably easier than joining two pieces of worked canvas. (See rug section.) Only canvas of the same mesh and weight can be joined. Using carpet thread, sew the two pieces of canvas together, leaving five-eighths of an inch seam allowance. Match up the two pieces mesh for mesh, and hole for hole. Then needlepoint right over the seam just as if it were not there, being careful not to catch up the seam allowance in your stitches. When the project is finished open the seam flat and loosely stitch it down. If you are joining penelope canvas make sure you have the warp and woof threads all going in the same direction on both pieces. It's a good idea to machine stitch the edges you plan to join about a quarter of an inch from the edge. When joining corners they have to be matched up very carefully, and

Detail of the War Memorial tapestry, National Cathedral, Washington, D. C. A large tree bears the seals of the fifty states. The emblems of the five services have also been worked into the design. Each state seal was appliquéed by the tying-in method onto the background canvas.

the joining almost always shows. The edges have to be mitred back, it is a very tricky joining to do.

Strengthening a Weak Spot   The reasons for strengthening would be a weak split thread, or a cut thread from careless stitch removal. Cut a piece of matching canvas one-half inch larger than the area that needs strengthening. Loosely baste the patch to the wrong side of the canvas with a piece of wool. Match up the mesh as carefully as you can. Stitch right over the canvas, going through the patch's mesh too, just as though the patch were not there. When that area is completed, trim any canvas threads poking out from the back.

APPLIQUÉ

There are two reasons for appliquéing one piece of canvas to another: to give greater detail to one area such as the face of a figure or the petals of a flower; and to allow more than one person to work on a large project. An example of the latter is the War Memorial tapestry in the Washington Cathedral in Washington, D. C. The tapestry measures 9 by 12 feet. The large background pieces (sewn together when completed) showing the branches of a tree were worked by one group of individuals and the state seals which are appliquéed to the branches of the tree were worked by other individuals. The seals were tied in.

Appliqué is generally done on mono-canvas since the same idea may be achieved on penelope by just separating the mesh and using petit point for the details. However, on some old canvases penelope was used for the gros point and petit point and then gauze was appliquéed to give even greater detail.

If you are appliquéing two pieces of the same mesh canvas the appliqué piece must be the exact mesh count as the blank space it will fill. Thus a piece which is fourteen mesh by twelve mesh will fit into a blank space fourteen mesh by twelve mesh. If the mesh of the

The shepherdess and her dog are petit point, her face and arms were done on gauze and then appliquéed on.

Detail of the shepherdess showing the gauze appliqué, the petit point and the gros point. She wears a hair ribbon worked in silk. Her eyelashes and eyebrows were embroidered in over the half cross stitches.

147

two pieces of canvas do not match you must rely on exact linear measurement. Make sure that all the stitches of the appliqué will be going in the same direction as the background canvas.

The Sew-on Method of Appliqué Block the pieces before sewing them together. If the piece to be appliquéed is large enough machine stitch with fine thread around the very edge of the worked area. The pieces must fit exactly. Trim the edge of the appliqué to a quarter of an inch from the worked area. With a single thread of silk, or matching cotton thread, stitch the excess quarter of an inch to the back of the worked area, allowing no stitches to show through to the front. Mitre sharp corners if necessary. With a single thread of silk, baste the piece lightly into place. Using a single thread of the same color that edges the appliqué, blind stitch the appliqué to the canvas. Your needle will

Canvas unraveled, in preparation for tying-in to background canvas

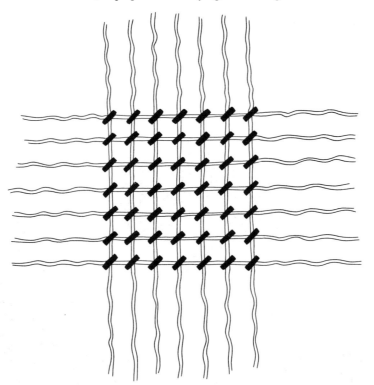

be going through worked appliqué to bare canvas, your fingernails will help in holding the piece into place. Sometimes the threads of the canvas or gauze of the appliquéed piece poke through the worked area to the front. There is nothing that you can do to prevent this without adding bulk to the appliqué.

The Tie-in Method   This is the method to use for pieces of canvas of the same mesh, or of no more than four mesh difference. Tying in pieces that have a difference of more than four mesh produces botchy looking appliqué. The piece to be appliquéed must have a border of at least two inches of unworked canvas on all sides. Unravel the bare canvas border. When unravelled the piece will have a fringe of canvas threads around it similar to the fringe on a rug. Using a short blunt needle, thread one of the canvas fringe into the background canvas. Put the needle into the nearest completed stitch hole, pull the thread through, free the needle and go to the very next canvas thread and thread it into the background canvas. Do about an inch this way and then stop to tie the canvas threads together by pairs. If the mesh are not the same you will have to draw two threads through one hole in some places, space them evenly. Don't pull too hard on the individual canvas threads or they will pull right through and out of the canvas all together! Press with a damp cloth or steam iron when finished. If the canvases are not too stretched out of shape before appliquéing they may be blocked after appliquéing.

CANVAS AND WOOL

Art needlework stores generally have a good supply of ten mesh to the inch penelope by the yard. They also have tapestry wool and possibly crewel wool. Paternayan wool made by the Paternayan Brothers, Inc. (wholesalers) of 312 East 95th Street, New York 28, New York, was used for all of the testing in this book. They supply the following stores with Persian and crewel wool and some they also supply with their tapestry and rug wool.

Alice Maynard
558 Madison Avenue
New York 22, New York

The Yarn Depot, Inc.
545 Sutter Street
San Francisco, California

Theodore E. Doelger, Inc.
P. O. Box 126
Blauvelt, New York

The American Needlework Center, Inc.
1729-A 20th Street, N. W.
Washington 9, D. C.

Petit Point supplies can be purchased from:

C. R. Meissner Co., Inc.
22 East 29th Street
New York 16, New York

Woolcraft Limited
#4 Trading Company Bldg.
Regina, Saskatchewan, Canada

You will find all these firms *most* helpful and cooperative.

FRAMES

Needlepoint frames may be purchased from:

Bamberger's
Dept. 14 M-A
Newark 1, New Jersey.

Rug hooking frames may be purchased anywhere rug hooking wool is sold.

HANDBAG FINISHING

Handbag finishing with leather trim on a metal frame can be done by:

Martha Klein
3785 Broadway
New York 32, New York

Carrol, Alice, *The Good Housekeeping Needlecraft Encyclopedia* New York, Rinehart, 1947

Dean, Beryl, *Ecclesiastical Embroidery,* London, B. T. Batsford, Ltd., 1958

de Dillmont, Therese, *Encyclopedia of Needlework,* France, D. M. C. Library

Hope, Mrs. George Curling, *My Working Friend,* London, W. H. Collingridge, circa 1850

Hughes, Therle, *English Domestic Needlework,* New York, Macmillan, 1961

Lent, D. Geneva, *Needlepoint as a Hobby,* New York, Harpers, 1942

Lewis, Griselda, (editor) *Handbook of Crafts,* London, E. Hulton & Co., Ltd., 1960

Picken, Mary Brooks; White, Doris, *Needlepoint Made Easy,* New York, Harpers, 1955

Spears, Ruth Wyeth, *The Work Basket Embroidery Book,* New York, M. Barrows, 1941

Thesiger, Ernest, *Adventures in Embroidery,* New York, Studio Books, 1941

Parentheses indicate an illustration (not color)

Italics indicate main mention and proper name

PICTURE ACKNOWLEDGMENTS

5. (Title Page). Collection of Irwin Untermyer

14. Top belt: courtesy, Mrs. W. Gilman Low; other belts and pouch: courtesy, Mrs. Charles W. Parker; billfold and bags: courtesy, Miss Elinor M. Parker; slippers designed by Alice Maynard, worked by Miss Parker: courtesy, Mr. George McKay Schieffelin

15. Courtesy, Mrs. Lewis B. Hershey

19. Photograph by Lee Salsbery

20. Courtesy, The Smithsonian Institution

21. Courtesy, Mrs. George Maurice Morris. Photograph by Lee Salsbery

22. Courtesy, Chelsea Old Church, London. Photograph by W. Churcher

24. Photograph by Lee Salsbery

26. Courtesy, The Smithsonian Institution

27. Courtesy, The Smithsonian Institution

28. Courtesy, The Metropolitan Museum of Art, Gift of Mary S. Harkness, 1948, in memory of her husband, Edward S. Harkness

29. Courtesy, The Metropolitan Museum of Art, Rogers Fund, 1948

31. Photograph by Lee Salsbery

32. Photograph by Lee Salsbery

33. National Trust for Historic Preservation–Woodlawn Plantation Collection, Mount Vernon, Virginia. Photograph by Lee Salsbery

36. Courtesy, Mr. Jay Clark IV, worked by his mother, Mrs. Ida-Hays McCormick Wende. Photograph by Lee Salsbery

37. Courtesy, Mrs. Thomas P. Dillon, worked by her mother, Mrs. Edith Pratt Maxwell. Photograph by Lee Salsbery

38. Courtesy, Colonial Williamsburg.

39. *Top:* Courtesy, The Metropolitan Museum of Art, Gift of R. Thornton Wilson, 1943, in memory of Florence Ellsworth; *bottom:* courtesy, The Cooper Union Museum, New York

40. Photograph by Lee Salsbery

43. *Top and bottom:* courtesy, National Cathedral, Washington, D. C. Photographs by Lee Salsbery

44. *Top and bottom:* courtesy, Dr. Douglas Price. Photographs by Lee Salsbery

49. Photograph by Lee Salsbery

51. *Left:* card reproduced by permission of Hallmark; *right:* courtesy, Victor R. Forte Jr., worked by the author. Photograph by Lee Salsbery

55. Courtesy, The Smithsonian Institution

81. National Trust for Historic Preservation—Woodlawn Plantation Collection, Mount Vernon. Photograph by Lee Salsbery

87. Courtesy, The Metropolitan Museum of Art, Gift of Irwin Untermyer, 1953

89. Chair: courtesy, Dr. and Mrs. Henry L. Darner; bell pull: courtesy, Mrs. George Maurice Morris. Photographs by Lee Salsbery

94. Courtesy, Dr. Douglas Price. Photograph by Lee Salsbery

COLOR PLATES